The Right to
Home
School

*A Guide to the Law
on Parents' Rights
in Education*

The Right to
Home
School

*A Guide to the Law
on Parents' Rights
in Education*

Third Edition

Christopher J. Klicka
Senior Counsel of the Home School
Legal Defense Association

Carolina
Academic
Press

CAROLINA ACADEMIC PRESS
700 Kent Street
Durham, North Carolina 27701

Telephone (919) 489-7486
Fax (919) 493-5668
www.cap-press.com

Printed in the United States of America.

To my wife Tracy for her sacrificial support of me and my work and to my seven wonderful children Bethany, Megan, Jesse, Susanna, Charity, Amy, and John whom I love dearly.

Contents

Table of Cases

Preface

Home schooling is exactly what the name implies: a school in the home. The teachers in a home school are the parents, and these parents have a commitment to make the necessary career sacrifices in order to personally provide an education for their children. For the majority, their primary reason to home school is to teach their children Christian principles and give them a thorough education — a reaction to the steady academic and moral decline in the public schools. And home schooling works. Over nine state departments of education and numerous independent studies have found that, on the average, home schooled children score above average on standardized achievement tests. Numerous educational curricula and resources are readily available to families who home school. Furthermore, these home school students are being accepted into hundreds of universities across the country including Harvard, Yale and Princeton.

This success is achieved by home school parents even though over half have only a high school diploma. Their success with their children, along with hundreds of other studies, show there is no positive correlation between teacher qualifications and student performance. Their commitment to their children is the key to their success.

Furthermore, these home schooled children are protected from negative socialization, such as drugs, sexually transmitted diseases, and violence present in the public schools. Instead, the home schooled child is trained in the traditional values on which our country was founded, and their self esteem, which best determines the socialization of a child, is carefully nurtured.

Historically, home schooling was one of the major forms of education until the early 1900s. Hundreds of great leaders in America have been home schooled, including at least eleven presidents and Patrick Henry, John Marshall, John Stuart Mill, George Bernard Shaw, Thomas Edison, Pearl Buck, Mark Twain, Andrew Carnegie, George Patton and Douglas MacArthur.

Today, the number of home schooled students is estimated as high as 1.5 million. Since 1982, 35 states have specifically enacted laws to protect the constitutional rights of parents to teach their own children. Home schooling is not a passing fad. Home schooling works, and as it steadily grows, it will continue to promote academic excellence and graduate productive citizens many years ahead of their peers.

This book will discuss in detail the phenomena of home schooling, especially its impact on education law and parental rights. The following chapters will review scores and scores of home school cases which secured rights for home school parents throughout the country. This book will also summarize the statutory trend to deregulate home schooling, which is encouraging families to continue this highly successful form of education.

Christopher J. Klicka
April, 2001

The Right to

Home School

A Guide to the Law on Parents' Rights in Education

1 What Is Home Schooling?[1]

Home schooling is exactly what the name implies: a school in the home. The Illinois Supreme Court defined a school as "a place where instruction is imparted to the young."[2] The teachers in a home school are usually the parents, and it is estimated that at least 50% of the parents have only a high school diploma.[3] One element all the home school parents seem to have in common is a commitment to make the necessary sacrifices to personally provide an education for their children.

---

1. For a complete handbook on home schooling, consult Christopher Klicka, *Home Schooling: The Right Choice*, (Twin Sisters, Oregon: Loyal Publishing). *The Right Choice* describes the history of home schooling in America, how to home school, home schooling in the military, failures of public schools, benefits of home schooling, how to lobby, the home school hall of fame and much more.

2. *People* v. *Levisen*, 404 Il. 574, 90 N.E.2d 213, (1950). *Black's Law Dictionary* defines the term "school" as "an institution **or place** for instruction or education."

3. In July, 1986, Lauri Scogin, B.S., M.A., an independent educational research consultant, did a random survey of 300 home school families from across the states and found that 45% of the parents had a college degree or higher, 50% had high school diplomas, and the remainder had below high school. See "Home Schoolers Excel," *The Home School Court Report*, Vol. 3, No.1, January-February, 1987.

This finding is supported by a study of 199 home schoolers conducted by Donald Wynn, Sr. which found that 54% of home school parents had college degrees or higher. See "A Study of the Development of Home Schools As an Alternative to Public School Education," as appeared in the *Home School Researcher*, (Seattle: Home School Researcher, 1989), Vol. 5, No. 1, p. 18.

With the advent of the public school system and the passage of compulsory attendance laws in all fifty states during the early 1900s, home schooling virtually died out. Beginning in the 1980s, the number of home schooled students rose again with estimates ranging as high as 1.2 million being home schooled nationwide.[4] By the year 2000, the Home School Legal Defense Association estimated over 2 million students were taught at home. The primary reason that most of these parents have chosen to home school is religious. In fact, approximately 85 percent of the home schooling families are doing so for religious reasons.[5] One study of over 2000 home school families found 93.8% of the fathers and 96.4% of the mothers described themselves as being "born again" Christians.[6] These parents believe that God has given them the responsibility and the authority to educate their children. Since they are called by God to be the primary teachers of their children and to apply God's Word to each and every subject, they believe it would be a sin for them to delegate this authority to another school system.[7]

4. John Naisbett, *Megatrends: Ten New Directions Transforming Our Lives* (New York: Warner Books, 1982) 144 and the Hewitt-Moore Research Foundation study published in "On Home Schooling Figures and Scores," *The Family Report*, Washougal, WA, Vol. 4, No. 2, March-April 1986. Also see "Shunning the Schools, More Parents Teach Their Kids at Home," *The Wall Street Journal*, October 6, 1986.

5. This conclusion has been drawn from the applications of over 70,000 home school families across the nation who have joined the Home School Legal Defense Association since 1985 and from conversations with state home school leaders.

Also the North Carolina Department of Education released a study for the 1988-89 school term and found that out of 1385 home schools registered with the state, 1085 designated themselves as "religious" schools. "North Carolina Home School Enrollment By Ages and Statewide Statistical History," (Raleigh, Division of Non-Public Education, December 1, 1989).

6. Dr. Brian Ray, "A Nationwide Study of Home Education: Family Characteristics, Legal Matters, and Student Achievement," National Home Education Research Institute, Seattle, Washington, 1990.

7. Many home school authors echo these profound, Christian beliefs concerning education which are commonly held throughout the home school movement. For example, see Blair Adams and Joel Stein, *Wisdom's Children*, (Austin,

A secondary reason parents offer is their concern over the academic and moral decline in the public schools.[8] They are dissatisfied and disappointed with the removal of God and religion from public schools[9] and the studies which have shown that more than 27 million illiterate children have graduated from the public schools in recent years.[10]

For example, John Taylor Gatto, recent New York Teacher of the Year quit after twenty-six years of teaching, because the public schools were a dismal failure. In an interview, Mr. Gatto said he quit because he didn't want to "hurt" kids anymore. He also said "government schooling ... kills the family by monopolizing the best times of childhood and by teaching disrespect for home and parents."[11] In an earlier speech on January 31, 1990 after accepting an award from the New York State Senate naming him "New York City Teacher of the Year," Gatto gave more details:

> Schools were designed by Horace Mann and by Sears and Harper of the University of Chicago and Thorndyke

---

TX: Truth Forum, 1989), pp. 88-130; Gregg Harris, *The Christian Home School* (Brentwood, TN: Wolgemuth & Hyatt, 1988), pp. 61-80; J. Richard Fugate, *Will Early Education Ruin Your Child?* (Tempe, AZ: Alpha Omega, 1990) pp. 3-13; Theodore Wade, Jr., *The Home School Manual* (Auburn, CA: Gazelle, 1991) pp. 177-186.

8. See note 5.

9. For documentation of the censorship of traditional moral and biblical values from public school textbooks, see Paul C. Vitz, "Religion and Traditional Values in Public School Textbooks: An Empirical Study," *Report of NIE Grant: Equity in Values Education: Do the Values Education Aspects of Public School Curricula Deal Fairly with Diverse Belief Systems?* (NIE 6-84-0012; Project No. 2-0099).

Also see generally David Barton, *America: To Pray or Not to Pray?* (Aledo, TX: David Barton, 1988).

10. The most significant government study that first revealed the deplorable condition of the modern public school system was performed by the National Commission on Excellence in Education entitled, *A Nation at Risk: The Imperative of Educational Reform*, (1982), reprinted in Congressional Record S6059 (daily ed. May 5, 1983).

11. Carol Innerst, "N.Y. Teacher of Year Walks Out on System," *The Washington Times*, October 22, 1991, p. A-1.

of Columbia Teacher's College and some other men to be instruments of scientific management of a mass population. Schools are intended to produce through the application of formulae, formulaic human beings whose behavior can be predicted and controlled . . . the products of schooling are, as I have said, irrelevant . . . useless to others and useless to themselves.[12]

We live in a time of great school crisis. We rank at the bottom of nineteen industrial nations in reading, writing, and arithmetic. At the very bottom. The world's narcotic economy is based upon our consumption of this commodity: If we didn't buy so many powdered dreams the business would collapse — and schools are an important sales outlet. Our teenage suicide rate is the highest in the world and suicidal kids are rich kids for the most part, not the poor. In Manhattan, 70% of all new marriages last less than five years. So something is wrong for sure . . . [13]

I don't think that we'll get rid of schools any time soon, certainly not in my lifetime, but if we're going to change what's rapidly becoming a disaster of ignorance we need to realize that the school institution "schools" very well but it does not "educate" — that's inherent in the design of the thing. It's not the fault of bad teachers or too little money spent. It's just impossible for education and schooling ever to be the same thing.[14]

The daily misery around us is, I think, in large measure caused by the fact that, as Paul Goodman put it thirty years ago, we force children to grow up absurd. Any reform in schooling has to deal with its absurdities.

It is absurd and anti-life to be part of a system that compels you to sit in confinement with people of exactly the same age and social class. That system effectively cuts you off from the immense diversity of life and the syner-

---

12. John Taylor Gatto, *Dumbing Us Down*, (Philadelphia, PA: New Society Publishers, 1992), p. 26.

13. *Ibid.*, p. 23-24.

14. *Ibid.*, p. 26.

gy of variety; indeed it cuts you off from your own past and future, sealing you in a continuous present much the same way television does...

Two institutions at present control our children's lives-television and schooling in that order, both of these reduce the real world of wisdom, fortitude, temperance, and justice to a never-ending, non-stop abstraction. In centuries past the time of the child and adolescent would be occupied in real work, real charity, real adventures, and the realistic search for mentors who might teach what you really wanted to learn. A great deal of time was spent in community pursuits, practicing affection, meeting and studying every level of the community, learning how to make a home and dozens of other tasks necessary to become a whole man or a woman.[15]

John Taylor Gatto and hundreds of studies all recognize that the public schools are in sad shape.

In another example, psychologist W. R. Coulson, who holds a doctorate in Philosophy from the University of Notre Dame and another in Counseling Psychology from the University of California at Berkeley, was more critical than even Gatto. During the 1960s, Coulson was an associate of Carl Rogers and Abraham Maslow, gurus to a generation of psychologists and educators and both winners of the "Humanist of the Year Award." It is interesting to note that both Rogers and Maslow finally acknowledged the educational failure of encounter groups, sensitivity training, and values clarification.

Coulson in an interview remarks:

American education has experienced a 'meltdown' because it has 'wimped out on substance'. Teachers have 'lost their nerve.' Furthermore, the public schools are highly secularized and seek to 'convert' children to a 'humanistic' ethic. Moreover, the sex and anti-drug education the

---

15. *Ibid.*, p. 28.

schools dish out only encourages young people to have sex and use drugs...Coulson believes that we have 'given in' to the 'religion of psychology,' particularly in the area of education, which has become too therapeutic.' He is critical of 'lifestyle' programs which take away from academic achievement. The educational system has in his view fallen into such bogus offerings as 'visualization' and 'relaxation' because today's teachers often can't deliver the academic goods. 'Teachers are not learning to teach,' Coulson says, but instead are becoming 'facilitators.' In that capacity, they 'make students feel good about their disablement.'

Such trends Coulson sees has proceeding not just from prominent humanist John Dewey but from Horace Mann and the fathers of mass education in America. The system, he says is essentially 'unitarianism in the classroom.' What the schools are forking out now is not only religious, Coulson contends, but it is 'religious trash' and in that judgment he is not alone.[16]

Furthermore, a highly reputed educational journal analyzes one of the most destructive aspects of the modern public schools' instruction which is exposed by Coulson and Gatto above:

Values clarification appears, at least by default, to hold the view that all values are equally valid...The moral point of view imbedded in values clarification is that of the ethical relativist. In its simplest definition, ethical relativism holds that one person's views are as good as another's; everyone is entitled to his own morality, and when it comes to morality, there is no way of showing one opinion is better than the other. The fundamental objection to ethical relativism is that it can be used to justify virtually any activity in which an individual or society wishes to engage.[17]

---

16. "Psychologist Unloads on Religious Trash in Nations Schools," *World*, October 27, 1990, p. 10. This is based on an interview with W. R. Coulson.

17. Alan B. Lockwood, "Values Clarification," *Teachers College Record*, Vol. 77, No. 1 (September 1977), pp. 46-47.

Parents who choose to home school often express their objections to the public schools in similar terms. A professor at Pepperdine University condemned the public school product:

> I believe that the decline in education is probably responsible for the widespread use of drugs. To live in the midst of a civilized society with a level of knowledge closer perhaps to that of primitive man than to what a civilized adult requires (which, regrettably, is the intellectual state of many of today's students and graduates) must be a terrifying experience, urgently calling for some kind of relief, and drugs may appear to many to be the solution...
>
> This is no longer an educational system. Its character has been completely transformed and it now clearly reveals itself to be what for many decades it has been in the process of becoming: namely an agency working for the barbarization of youth.[18]

Home schooling parents simply want the choice to protect their children from becoming a one of these statistics of academic or moral failure. They want the right to choose to teach their children themselves.

At first the public was generally against home schooling. They claimed that home schooling would hamper a child's growth and parents with merely a high school diploma could never successfully teach their children. Home schoolers proved them wrong. Home schooling does work, and the end product is children who score above average on standardized achievement tests and who are readily accepted into universities. The court- recognized interest of the state in the education of children is easily satisfied by home schooled children.

---

18. George Reisman, Professor of Economics, Pepperdine University, *The Intellectual Activist*, as quoted in the "Blumenfeld Education Letter," (Boise, Idaho, August 1990), p. 8.

Can Home School Students Compete Academically?

Many studies over the last two decades have established the academic excellence of home schooled children. Not only can home schooled students compete with children in public school, they excel, generally performing much better than the average student. Below is a brief summary of some of these studies.

Independent Evaluations of Home Schooling

In South Carolina, the National Center for Home Education did a survey of 65 home school students and found that the average scores on the Comprehensive Test of Basic Skills were 30 percentile points higher than national public school averages. In math, 92 percent of the home school students scored above grade level, and 93 percent of the home school students are at or above grade level in reading. These impressive scores are "being achieved in a state where public school SAT scores are next-to-last in national rankings."[19]

Dr. Brian Ray, president of the Home Education Research Institute reviewed over 65 studies concerning home education. He found that home schoolers were performing at or above average on testing.[20]

In Pennsylvania, 171 home schooled students took the CTBS Standardized Achievement test. The tests were all administered in group settings by Pennsylvania certified teachers. The middle reading score was the 89th percentile, and the middle math score was the 72nd percentile. The middle science score was the 87th percentile, and the middle social studies score was the 81st percentile.

---

19. Statistics compiled by the National Center For Home Education, P.O. Box 125, Paeonian Springs, VA 20129 in 1990.

20. Brian Ray, *Education and Urban Society*, Vol. 21, No.1, November, 1988 16-31 (Newbury Park, CA).

A survey was conducted of the home school families who participated in this testing which found that the average student spent only 16 hours per week in formal schooling (i.e. structured lessons preplanned by either the parent or a provider of educational materials).[21]

In 1982, Dr. Raymond Moore studied several thousand home schooled children throughout the United States. His research found that these children have been performing, on the average, in the 75th to the 95th percentile on Stanford and Iowa Achievement Tests.[22] Additionally, Dr. Moore did a study of home schooled children whose parents were criminally charged for exercising their right to teach their own children. He found that the children scored on the average in the 80th percentile.[23]

In 1990, the National Home Education Research Institute issued a report entitled "A Nationwide Study of Home Education: Family Characteristics, Legal Matters, and Student Achievement." This was a study of over 2163 home schooling families.

The study found that the *average* scores of the home school students were at or above the 80th percentile in all categories. The

21. "PA Homeschooled Students Score High!," article which appeared in "Pennsylvania Homeschoolers" newsletter, Fall 1990, Issue #33, Kittanning, PA p1.

22. Moore, Raymond, "Research and Common Sense: Therapies for Our Home Schools," *Teachers College Record*, Columbia University, Vol. 84, No. 2, 1982, 372.

For further documentation of the academic success of home schooling see Linden, N.J. "An Investigation of Alternative Education: Home Schooling." Ph.D. dissertation, East Texas State University, 1983.

Also see Brian Ray, "A Comparison of Home Schooling and Conventional Schooling: With a Focus on Learner Outcomes, (Ph.D. diss., Oregon State University, 1986). The author concluded, based on reviewing eleven studies which addressed the achievement of home school children, home schoolers were matching, and in many cases, excelling the average school achievement.

23. "Home Schooling: An Idea Whose Time Has Returned," *Human Events*, September 15, 1984.

home schoolers' national percentile mean was 84 for reading, 80 for language, 81 for math, 84 for science, and 83 for social studies.

The research revealed that there was no positive correlation between state regulation of home schools and the home-schooled students' performance. The study compared home schoolers in three groups of states representing various levels of regulation. Group 1 represented the most restrictive states such as Michigan; Group 2 represented slightly less restrictive states including North Dakota; and Group 3 represented unregulated states such as Texas and California. The Institute concluded:

> ...*no* difference was found in the achievement scores of students between the three groups which represent various degrees of state regulation of home education.... It was found that students in all three regulation groups scored on the average at or above the 76th percentile in the three areas examined: total reading, total math, and total language. These findings in conjunction with others described in this section, do *not* support the idea that state regulation and compliance on the part of home education families assures successful student achievement.[24]

In 1997, a study of 5,402 home school students from 1657 families was released. It was entitled, *Strengths of Their own: Home Schoolers Across America.* The study demonstrated that home schoolers, on the average, out-performed their counterparts in the public schools by 30 to 37 percentile points in all subjects. A significant finding when analyzing the data for 8th graders was the evidence that home schoolers who are home schooled two or more years score substantially higher than students who have been home schooled one year or less. The new home schoolers were scoring on the average in the 59th percentile compared to students home

---

24. Dr. Brian Ray, "A Nationwide Study of Home Education: Family Characteristics, Legal Matters, and Student Achievement," National Home Education Research Institute, Seattle, WA, 1990, p. 53-54.

schooled the last two or more years who scored between the 86th and 92nd percentile.[1]

This was confirmed in another study by Dr. Larry Rudner of 20,760 home schooled students which found the home schoolers who have home schooled all their school-aged years had the highest academic achievement. This was especially apparent in the higher grades.[2] This is a good encouragement to families to catch the long-range vision and home school through high school.

Another important finding of *Strengths of Their Own* was that race of the student does not make any difference. There was no significant difference between minority and white home schooled students. For example, in grades K-12, both white and minority students scored, on the average, in the 87th percentile. In math, whites scored in the 82nd percentile while minorities scored in the 77th percentile. In the public schools, however, there is a sharp contrast. White public school eighth grade students nationally scored in the 58th percentile in the math and the 57th percentile in reading. Black eighth grade students, on the other hand, scored on the average at the 24th percentile in math and the 28th percentile in reading. Hispanics scored at the 28th percentile in math and the 28th percentile in reading.[3]

1. Dr. Brian Ray, *Strengths of Their Own: Home Schoolers Across America*, National Home Education Research Institute, Salem, OR, 1997.

2. Lawrence M. Rudner, Ph.D., Director of the ERIC Clearing House on Assessment and Evaluation, *Home Schooling Works: The Scholastic Achievement and Demographic Characteristics of Home School Students in 1998*, published by the Home School Legal Defense Association, Purcellville, VA 20134, www.hslda.org. ERIC is sponsored by the National Library Services of the U.S. Department of Education.

3. Dr. Brian Ray, *Strengths of Their Own: Home Schoolers Across America*, National Home Education Research Institute, Salem, OR, 1997.

State Department of Education Statistics on Home Schoolers

Several state departments of education or local school districts have also gathered statistics on the academic progress of home schooled children.

In the spring of 1987, the Tennessee Department of Education found that home schooled children in 2nd grade, on the average, scored in the 93rd percentile while their public school counterparts, on the average, scored in the 62nd percentile on the Stanford Achievement test. Children in third grade scored, on the average, in the 90th percentile in reading on another standardized test and the public school students scored in the 78 percentile. In math, the third grade home schooled children scored, on the average, in the 87th percentile while their public school counterparts scored in the 80th percentile. In eighth grade, the home schooled students scored, on the average, in the 87th percentile in reading and in 71st percentile in math while their public school counterparts scored in the 75th percentile in reading and the 69th percentile in math.[28]

Similarly, in 1986, the State Department of Education in Alaska which had surveyed home schooled children's test results every other year since 1981, found home schooled children to be scoring approximately 16 percentage points higher, on the average, than the children of the same grades in conventional schools.[29] In Oregon, the State Department of Education compiled test score statistics for 1658 home schooled children in 1988 and found that 51 percent of the children scored above the 71st percentile and 73 percent scored above the 51st percentile.[30]

---

28. Office of the Commissioner, Tennessee Department of Education, *Home School Student Test Results: 1986 and 1987*, (Nashville, 1987).

29. *Method: Alaska Perspectives*, Vol. 7, No.1 (Juneau, Alaska Dept. of Education, 1986).

30. "March 1, 1988 Oregon Home School Data Report," *Line Upon Line*, Beaverton, OR, Dec. 1988, Vol. 11, No. 5. The date was compiled from information submitted from the Educational Service District and County Units in Ore-

In North Carolina, the Division of Non-Public Education compiled test results of 2,144 home school students in grades K-12. Of the 1,061 home school students taking the California Achievement Test, they scored, on the average, at the 73rd percentile on the total battery of tests: 80th percentile in reading, 72nd percentile in language, and the 71st percentile in math.

The 755 home school students who took the Iowa Basic Skills test scored at the 80th percentile in the total battery of tests: 81st percentile in reading, 77th percentile in language, and 77th percentile in math. The remaining students who took the Stanford, scored, on the average, in the 73th percentile in the whole battery.[31]

In Arkansas, for the 1987-88 school term, home school children, on the average, scored in the 75th percentile on the Metropolitan Achievement Test 6. They out-scored public school children in every subject (Reading, Math, Language, Science, and Social Studies) and at every grade level. For example, at the 10th grade level public school children scored an average of 53rd percentile in social studies while home school children scored at the 73rd percentile. In science, an area in which home schoolers are often criticized for lack of facilities, the home schoolers scored, on the average, 85th percentile in fourth grade, 73rd percentile in seventh grade, and 65th percentile in tenth grade. The public school students, on the other hand, scored much lower in science: 66th percentile in fourth grade, 62nd percentile in seventh, and 53rd percentile in tenth.[32]

gon between September 1987 and March 1988.

Office of Policy and Program Development, Oregon Department of Education, Les Marten, *December 1, 1986, Home School Data Report*, (Salem, 1986) showed in 1986 that of 1121 home schoolers, 76 percent were above the 50 percentile.

31. "North Carolina Home School Nationally Standardized Achievement Test Results 88-89 School Term," (Raleigh, Office of the Governor, Division of Non-Public Education, Dec. 1, 1989).

32. "Standardized Test Results," *Update*, (Little Rock, Arkansas Christian Home Education Association, Sept. 1988), Vol. 7, No. 1.

According to the Arizona State Department of Education, 1,123 home schooled children in grades 1-9, on the average, scored *above* grade level in reading, language arts, and math on standardized tests for the 1988-89 school year. Four grades tested were a full grade level ahead.[33]

In Nebraska, out of 259 home schooled children who returned to public or non-public schools, 134 of them were automatically placed in their grade level according to their age without testing. Of the remaining who were given entrance tests, 33 were above grade level, 43 were at grade level and 29 were below grade level. Approximately 88 percent of the returning students were at or above grade level after being home schooled for a period of time. This survey resulted from the responses of 429 accredited schools.[34]

Conclusion of the Studies: Home Schooling Works

These statistics point to one conclusion: home schooling works. Even many of the State Departments of Education, which are generally biased in favor of the public school system, cannot argue with these facts. Not only does home schooling work, but it works without the myriad of state controls and accreditation standards imposed on the public schools.

This newsletter reported on test results compiled by the Arkansas Department of Education of 760 home schooled students.

33. Arizona Department of Education, *Students Taught at Home 1989 Average Grade Equivalents*, compiled by Steve Stephens, State Testing Coordinator, July 1989.

For earlier statistics for Arizona home schoolers success on standardized tests see article by Patricia Lines, "States Should Help, Not Hinder, Parents' Home Schooling Efforts," *Education Week*, May 15, 1985.

34. "Grade Level Placement of Rule 13 Students Returning to Approved or Accredited Schools" *Dateline: Education*, June, 1989.

Home School Students Accepted into Colleges and Universities

As a result of the excellent academic performance of home schoolers and high SAT scores, children who have been home schooled have had little difficulty getting into colleges and universities. Home schooled students have been accepted in Harvard, Yale, Princeton and nearly every college in the United States. Colleges are streamlining their admission policies, offering home school scholarships and actively recruiting home school graduates. Internal surveys reveal that the average grade point average of home schoolers is above the student body GPA average. Appendix I gives a detailed summary of the evidence demonstrating the success of home schoolers in college.

Are Home Schooled Children Socialized?

Academically, the home schoolers have generally excelled, but some critics have continued to challenge them on an apparent "lack of socialization." This problem, however has been overcome by most home schoolers through heavy involvement in church youth groups, community activities, music and art lessons, little league sports participation, YMCA, singing groups, activities with neighborhood children, academic contests (spelling bees, orations, creative and research papers), and regular involvement in field trips.

In nearly every community throughout the country, local "home school support groups" have been formed in addition to the state-wide home school associations. In many areas these local support groups sponsor weekly and monthly activities for the home school students, including physical education classes, special speakers, sports, 4H activities, camping, and trips to museums, industries, farms, parks, historic sites, and hundreds of other activities. The state home school associations generally sponsor a major conference home school children can attend. The older children speak, assemble year books, and perform graduation ceremonies for eighth and twelfth grades at these conferences. A review of the state home school association and local support group newsletters is a testimony to this fact: home school families, as a whole, do not raise their children in social isolation.[35]

In addition, several studies have been done to measure home schoolers' "self-concept," which is the key objective indicator for establishing a child's self esteem. A child's degree of self esteem, of course, is the best objective measurement of his ability to successfully interact on a social level. One such study was conducted using the Piers-Harris Children's Self-Concept Scale to evaluate 224 home schooled children. The study found that one half of the children scored above the 90th percentile and only 10.3% scored below the national average.[36]

Thomas Smedley prepared a master's thesis for Radford University of Virginia on "The Socialization of Home School Children." Smedley used the Vineland Adaptive Behavior Scales to evaluate the social maturity of twenty home-schooled children and thirteen demographically matched public school children. The communication skills, socialization, and daily living skills were evaluated. These scores were combined into the "Adoptive Behavior Composite" which reflects the general maturity of each subject.

Smedley had this information processed using the statistical program for the social sciences, and the results demonstrated that the home-schooled children were better socialized and more mature than the children in the public school. The home-schooled children

---

35. Meighan, R. "Political Consciousness and Home-Based Education," *Educational Review* 36(1984):165-73.

36. Taylor, John Wesley, *Self-Concept in Home Schooling Children*, Ann Arbor, MI, University Microfilms International, Order No. DA8624219. This study was done as part of a dissertation at Andrews University. The results of the testing of the 224 home schooled students was compared to the testing results of 1,183 conventionally schooled children.

scored in the 84th percentile while the matched sample of public school children only scored in the 27th percentile. Smedley further found:

> In the public school system, children are socialized horizontally, and temporarily, into conformity with their immediate peers. Home educators seek to socialize their children vertically, toward responsibility, service, and adulthood, with an eye on eternity."[37]

In another 1992 study, Dr. Larry Shyers compared behaviors and social development test scores of two groups of seventy children ages eight to ten. One group was being educated at home while the other group attended public and private schools. He found that the home-schooled children did not lag behind children attending public or private schools in social development.

Dr. Shyers further discovered that the home-schooled children had consistently fewer behavioral problems. The study indicated that home-schooled children behave better because they tend to imitate their parents while conventionally-schooled children model themselves after their peers. Shyers states:

> The results seem to show that a child's social development depends *more on adult contact* and less on contact with other children as previously thought.[38]

Another benefit from home school socialization is that the child can be protected from the negative socialization and peer pressure, such as rebellious attitudes, immaturity, immorality, drugs, and

---

37. Thomas C. Smedley, M.S., "Socialization of Home Schooled Children: A Communication Approach," thesis submitted and approved for Master of Science in Corporate and Professional Communication, Radford University, Radford, Virginia, May 1992. (Unpublished.)

38. Dr. Larry Shyers, "Comparison of Social Adjustment Between Home and Traditionally Schooled Students," unpublished doctoral dissertation at University of Florida's College of Education, 1992. Dr. Shyers is a psychotherapist who is the Chairman of the Florida Board of Clinical Social Work, Marriage and Family Therapy, and Mental Health Counseling.

violent behavior. This is becoming more of a factor as the crime rate continues to soar in the public schools.

Other Benefits of Home Schooling

There are numerous benefits to home schooling, in addition to having literate children who can be productive members of society.

A common difference between public schools and home schools is the amount of time parents need to spend per week instructing their children. It is clear that one-on-one instruction or parental tutoring is far more efficient than the time spent in institutional schools. As a result, the average home schooler only needs to spend, on the average, two to three hours per day receiving formal instruction. Furthermore, unlimited learning can take place beyond formal instruction by spending "time on task" with various projects and 'hands-on" experiences.

Richard Rossmiller of the University of Wisconsin studied elementary and secondary students throughout the country and discovered some interesting facts on how much time is wasted each year in institutional schools. According to his research, the typical student annually spends 367 hours (more than two hours a day) in activities such as lunch, recess, attendance-taking and class changing, and 66 hours in "process activities" during which teachers answer questions, distribute material and discipline students. In addition, the average pupil is absent from the classroom approximately 108 hours annually and loses about 54 hours to inclement weather, employee strikes, and teacher conferences.[39]

This study further documents the differences between the tutorial method (home schooling) and the institutional school. From a legal perspective, home schools should not be required to fulfill

---

39. "Home Schoolers Need Less Time," *Home School Court Report*, Vol. 4, No. 2, Spring 1988, 5.

institutional schools' hourly requirements without taking into account the inefficient use of time in the classroom.

Other benefits of home schooling include one-on-one instruction where the parent can develop his child's gifts and overcome the child's weaknesses. This can be done much more accurately and in much less time than in the conventional schools. Gifted children are free to excel, and slower students are not left behind.

Home Schooling Continues to Become More Popular

One of the largest studies was released by the National Center of Home Education on November 10, 1994. According to these standardized test results (provided by the Riverside Publishing Company) of 16,311 home school students from all 50 states K–12, the nationwide average for home school students is at the 77th percentile of the basic battery of the Iowa Test of Basic Skills. In reading, the home schoolers' nationwide grand mean is at the 79th percentile. This means, of course, that the home school students perform better in reading than 79% of the sample population on whom the test was normed. In the area of language arts and math, the typical home schooler scored in the 73rd percentile.

These 16,311 home school students' scores were not self-selected by parents or anyone else. They represent all the home schoolers, whose tests were scored through the Riverside Publishing Company. It is important to note that this roll-up of home school achievement test scores demonstrates that 54.7% of the students in grades K–12 are achieving individual scores in the top quarter of the population of students in the United States. This figure is more than double the number of conventional school students who score in the top quarter.[40]

---

40. This study was released by the National Center of Home Education, November 1994, Purcellville, VA.

Home schooling has become widely accepted. In January 1994, a front page article in *USA Today* recognized home schooling as one of several major trends of the 1990s that will take our nation into the 21st century. Overall, the success of home schoolers seems to be due to one-to-one instruction, tailoring instruction to the needs and ability of each individual child, more individual responses, and an absence of negative socialization pressure. These academic successes continue to fuel the rapid growth of the home schooling movement. As a result, the courts and legislatures have gradually changed laws to protect the rights of parents to choose to home school.

2 The Conflict: Parental Rights v. State Regulation

In spite of the impressive academic record of home schoolers and the numerous benefits of this type of tutorial education, certain groups, usually representing the educational establishment, continue to oppose home schooling in the legislatures. Home school families across the nation are also routinely harassed by their local school district or law enforcement officials.

Simply reviewing the cases involving home schoolers cited throughout this book clearly demonstrates that the conflict the state has with home schoolers has nothing to do with education. Home schoolers have consistently proved that their method works as documented in Chapter 1. In fact, in every single case in which the Home School Legal Defense Association has been involved since its inception in 1983, the children have performed at average or above average on standardized test scores. It is apparent the real issue involves who has the authority to mandate how the children must be educated. Do the parents or do the public schools have this authority?

The Clash Between Competing Financial Interests

The main opposition to home schooling is made up of public school officials and teachers' unions. This should be expected, since public school officials and teachers have a financial interest ($3000 to $4000 in tax monies per child for their school district from the state and federal governments) in whether or not home schoolers are allowed to exist. In fact, their jobs may even be on the line. This is a strong financial incentive, especially for small school districts, to disapprove home schools and get the children back in public school. This financial interest, of course, makes it very difficult for the school authorities to remain neutral when determining whether a home schooler should be allowed to freely operate. Chapter 8 discusses many examples of school officials who worried about the financial loss to their school district when children are taught at home. Chapter 8 also documents the amount of money each child is worth in state and federal tax dollars and constitutional implications.

The Clash Between Educational Philosophies

In addition, there is a philosophical reason for opposition to home schooling. Many public school officials actually believe they are the "guardians of the children," and as such they need sufficient controls over *all* the children within the boundaries of their school districts. They sincerely believe that since they often have seven years of higher education, they know what type of education is best for all children. They cannot understand how a mere parent can teach his children. Too many public school officials believe parents are inferior when it comes to training and educating children.

This combination of both the philosophy of control and the financial and competitive interest motivates public school authorities to do something about home schooling. Several of the powerful education unions and associations have begun vocalizing their opposition to home schooling in recent years. Following are several examples of the opposition's position reflecting the strong philosophical bias they have against home schooling.

The National Association of State Boards of Education (NASBE) issued their "Policy Update" in January, 1994.[1] Under "Components of Effective Home School Policies," NASBE stated:

> Whether home schooling is regulated through state board actions or state statutes, decision-makers should insure that policies have the following components: Specific provisions for insuring the competency of the instructor (e.g. teacher/instructor certification or certified teacher visits to home school site to observe instruction.... Assurance that policies with regards to home schooling are aligned with the state's current outcome-based standards and graduation requirements.

NASBE is not too friendly toward home schools and supports very restrictive regulations.

The National Education Association, a teachers' union with a budget exceeding $200 million dollars, has consistently opposed home schoolers in the legislatures. Below are excerpts from the 2000 resolutions of the NEA which are re-adopted annually.

> B-67. The National Education Association believes that home schooling programs cannot provide the student with a comprehensive education experience.
>
> The Association believes that, if parental preference home schooling study occurs, students enrolled must meet all state requirements. Instruction should be by persons who are licensed by the appropriate state education licensure agency, and a curriculum approved by the state department of education should be used.
>
> "The Association further believes that such programs should be limited to the children of the immediate family, with all expenses being borne by the parents."

---

1. "Policy Update," National Association of State Boards of Education, Vol. 2, No. 2, January 1994.

> "The Association believes that home schooled students should not participate in any extracurricular activities in the public school." (pre-K to 12).[2]

If the NEA had its way and every state required parents to be state certified and have their curriculum approved, at least 95% of the home schoolers in the country would be outlawed. On the issue of teacher certification, the NEA ignores the hundreds of studies which demonstrate no positive correlation between teacher qualifications and student performance as documented in Chapter 10. Of course, they also ignore the fact that parents have the right to choose to home school.

Annette Cootes of the Texas State Teachers Association declared, "My own personal opinion is that home schooling is a **form of child abuse** because you are isolating children from human interaction. I think home schoolers are doing a great discredit to their children."[3]

Another national organization is less polite concerning its opposition to home schooling. They would like to see home schooling completely prohibited.

The National Association of Elementary School Principals (NAESP) is urging local and state associations to promote legislative changes that will "enforce compulsory school attendance and prohibit at-home schooling as a substitute for compulsory school attendance." The NAESP's 1987–88, p.3, platform lists eight reasons why home schooling is inferior to the traditional classroom setting. The platform states:

> Such schooling:
> 1. Deprives the child of important social experiences; 2. Isolates students from other social/racial/ethnic groups: 3. Denies students the full range of curriculum experiences and materials; 4. May be provided by non-certified and unqualified persons; 5. Creates an additional burden on

---

2. "The 2000 Resolutions of the National Education Association."

3. Ann Zimmerman, "Is Anybody Home," *Dallas Observer*, November 21, 1991, p. 20.

administrators whose duties include the enforcement of compulsory school attendance laws; 6. May not permit effective assessment of academic standards of quality; 7. May violate health and safety standards; 8. May not provide the accurate diagnosis of and planning for meeting the needs of children with special talents, learning difficulties, and other conditions requiring atypical educational programs.

As far as this organization of public school officials is concerned, home schooling should be outlawed.

Another organization which is diametrically opposed to home schooling is the National Parent Teachers Association. At their 1987 national convention, they passed these resolutions:

> WHEREAS National PTA believes that all children should have access to equal educational opportunities; and
> WHEREAS, the National PTA has consistently supported a quality education for all students; and
> WHEREAS, the number of homeschools and other non-approved schools has increased significantly in the last five years; and
> WHEREAS, there are no uniform standards that home schools and other non-approved schools must meet, such as hours and days of instruction, curriculum, teacher certification, and reporting;
> NOW THEREFORE be it resolved that the National PTA encourages state PTAs to urge state boards of education and/or state legislators to require home and other non-approved schools to meet the same minimum educational standards as **public schools.**

This organization claims to be operating for parents.

Thomas Shannon, executive director of the National School Boards Association, in an interview, calls the home schooling trend, "a giant step backward into the 17th century." He stated further in the interview:

> We are very concerned that many parents who think they
> are qualified to teach their youngsters, simply are not....
> The youngsters are getting shortchanged.... Society ulti-
> mately has to pay for any mistakes, not to mention the loss
> of a child who might otherwise have made a maximum
> contribution.[4]

If he had not said he was talking about home schooling, it would
seem apparent he was describing the failure of the public school
system. There is certainly no documentation to support his assertion concerning home schooling.

In conclusion, it is clear the public education leaders are protecting their vested interest and are ignoring the academic statistics which expose the failure of the public schools and the consistent
success of home schoolers.

The Clash Between Parental Rights
and State Control

This bias against home schooling by the educational establishment and many school authorities results in numerous legal conflicts across the country each year.

For example, during one school year, nearly 2000 negative legal
contacts were handled by the Home School Legal Defense Association. These contacts involved various degrees of harassment,
ranging from actual or threatened prosecution to the attempted
imposition of restrictions in excess of the law.[5]

---

4. Mary Esch, "Home Schooling Good or Bad, More Parents Are Willing
to Try It," Associated Press, appeared in the *State Journal Register*, Springfield,
Il, June 30, 1991.

5. "The 1990–91 School Year in Review," *The Home School Court Report*,
July–August 1991, Vol. 7, No. 4, Home School Legal Defense Association,
Purcellville, VA, 540-338-5600. Also see back and later issues of the Home School
Court Report for a chronological account of harassment faced by home schoolers
around the nation.

Misapplication of the law even plagued the 35 states that had home school legislation. Single parents or parents with handicapped children received the worst treatment. For example, families were threatened with a termination of their right to home school by school districts trying to impose false notification deadlines, testing or evaluation procedures, curriculum requirements, or in some instances, qualification requirements.

In states where home schools either have to be approved by the school district or operate as a private school, the challenges were more intense. Many home schoolers were faced with illegal home visits, curriculum approval, and excessive qualification requirements. In several of these states the law is somewhat vague, which contributes to the arbitrary treatment of home schools.

The usual reason these home school families are harassed is connected to either the school official's philosophical bias and desire to control or the school district's financial interest.

Conclusion

Home education, one of the most important liberties, is protected by the First and Fourteenth Amendments as demonstrated in the following chapters. Home schooling is not for everybody, but it is for anybody. Anybody should have the right to choose to teach his own children. However, the opposition realizes the danger of this growing movement and seeks to regulate home schooling out of existence or at least into conformity.

3 The Nature and History of Parental Liberty in Education

During the first 250 years of the United States, education was not subject to the myriad regulations which presently conflict with the parents' right to control the **process** of their children's education. Parental liberty was held inviolate, and parents seriously heeded the rights and responsibilities of educating their children. Education was **not** a government responsibility, and it was left completely under the private control of parents and churches.

In fact, in *Abington v. Schempp*, the U. S. Supreme Court confirmed that education historically was privately-controlled, and public schooling, in the modern sense, was non-existent.

> In the North American Colonies, education was almost without exception under private sponsorship and supervision, frequently under control of the dominant Protestant sects.[1]

As a consequence of the pervasive church influence on American education, "the schools in their curriculum and methods were dominated by biblical ethics."[2] Similarly, the modern home school movement is comprised largely of fundamental Christians who hold

---

1. *Abington v. Schempp*, 374 U.S. 203 (1963), at 238, Note 7.
2. Whitehead, John, *The New Tyranny*, Ft. Lauderdale, Florida; Coral Ridge Publications p. 26.

sacred the biblical view of the family and practically apply God's principles to each and every subject. This fact that biblical theism dominated early American education and culture[3] explains why the present states' attempt to control and secularize private, Christian education and home schooling was non-existent back then. The Court in *Schempp* further comments,

> Education, as the framers knew it, was in the main confined to *private* schools more often than not under strictly *Sectarian supervision*. Only gradually did control of education pass largely to public officials.[4] (emphasis supplied).

For example, in 1647, the Massachusetts General Court passed the "Old Deluder Act" which required towns to maintain schools.[5] The primary goal of education, as defined in the act, was to instruct the child so he could comprehend the scripture. Although towns had to maintain schools, parents had the ultimate choice of how their children would be educated.

Another example of the fact that most schools were church-related and thus privately controlled can be found in *McCollum v. Board of Education*.[6] Justice Frankfurter delineates,

> Traditionally, organized education in the Western World was church education. It could hardly be otherwise when the education of children was primarily the study of the Word and ways of God. Even in the protestant countries ... the basis of education was largely the Bible, and its chief purpose the inculcation of piety. To the extent that the state

---

3. *Ibid.*, pp. 26-29.
4. *Schempp*, 374 U.S. 203 (1963), at 238. Even the public schools in existence during the early 1800s were locally controlled and nearly identical to the instruction found in private schools. Thomas Jefferson, as president of the Washington D.C. School Board, established the Bible and the Watts Hymnal as the principal books to be used for reading by the public school students. J.O. Wilson, *Public Schools of Washington* (Columbia Historical Society, 1897), p. 4.
5. See the *Laws and Liberties of Massachusetts*, 1648 ed. (Cambridge, 1929), p. 47.
6. *McCollum,* 333 U.S. 203 (1948) at 213-214.

intervened, it used its authority to further the aims of the Church.

The emigrants who came to these shores brought this view of education with them. Colonial schools certainly started with a religious orientation. When the problems of the early settlers of the Massachusetts Bay Colony revealed the need for common schools, the object was the defeat of "one chief project of that old deluder, satan, to keep men from the knowledge of the Scriptures."

Until the 1900s, this concept of parental liberty in education was unquestioned. One legal commentator documents:

> Historically, the education of children in the United States was a matter of parental discretion. Decisions to educate or not to educate, and the substance of that education—method and curriculum—were made by the parents as a right.[7]

This "preferred" position of the parents' duty and right in controlling the education of their children was securely established in the foundation of America's legal system and its roots in English common law, which was derived from the Bible.[8] One of the most influential common law sources on which the founders of our country relied was Sir William Blackstone's *Commentaries*. Blackstone recognized that the most important duty of parents to their chil-

---

7. Tobak & Zirkel, "Home Instruction: An Analysis of the Statutes and Case Law," 8 Univ. of Dayton Law Review at 13-14 (1982).

8. Constitutional scholar, John Whitehead in his book *Parents Rights* (Westchester, Il: Crossway Books, 1985), p. 85, explains the Christian foundation of common law:

> Essentially, the common law is an age-old doctrine that developed by way of court decisions which applied the principles of Christianity to everyday situations. Out of these cases, rules were established that governed future cases. This principle, with its origin in Europe... became part of American law.

Whitehead, in the same passage, also quotes law professor John C.H. Wu who stated: "... there can be no denying that the common law has one advantage over the legal system of any country: it was Christian from the very beginning of its history."

dren is that of giving them an education suitable to their station in life.[9] That duty, he admits, "was pointed out by reason."[10]

This function of the parent to control the education of his children has been a constitutionally recognized right in a long line of cases beginning with *Meyer v. Nebraska* in 1923.[11] A U.S. Supreme Court decision to protect parents' rights in education was not necessary prior to 1923, because there were hardly any compulsory attendance laws requiring children to attend public school. As soon as compulsory attendance laws were passed, however, the reduction of parental liberties began. Education became a state responsibility rather than a traditional parental responsibility. As experience teaches, whenever the state takes responsibility of any private sector, controls always follow. This was the way of education in America as it slowly began to be stifled by excessive government regulations.

Parental Liberty in Education is Derived From the 14th Amendment

Even though the Constitution does not specifically mention the right of parents to educate their children, that right is implied the Fourteenth Amendment. The Fourteenth Amendment guarantees all citizens the right to "liberty" which cannot be taken away without due process. The United States Supreme Court has determined that this guarantee of "liberty" includes "parental liberty." Based on this application of the Fourteenth Amendment, the Supreme Court has consistently held that parents have the "fundamental right" to "direct the upbringing and **education** of their children."[12]

---

9. Blackstone, *Blackstone's Commentaries*, New York: Augustus Kelley, (1969), Vol. II, p. 450.

10. *Id.*, at 450.

11. *Meyer v. Nebraska*, 262 U.S. 390 (1923).

12. See *Pierce* v. *Society of Sisters*, 268 U.S. 510, 534-35 (1925) and *Wisconsin* v. *Yoder*, 406 U.S. 205, 232 (1972).

The problem, however, is that the United States Supreme Court, while reasserting the parent's right to educate his children, also created an "interest" which the state now has in education. Consequently, with this "interest" in education comes government controls. The state's interest, as defined by the U.S. Supreme Court, is that children must grow up to be "literate" and "self-sufficient."[13]

Of course, the state, in order to protect its "interest" in education, tries to impose restrictive requirements such as teacher certification requirements, curriculum approval, home visits, and countless other controls on parents who are home schooling. The courts then determine who must give way: the state's interest in regulating education or the parents' fundamental right to educate their children in the manner they choose. Since this conflict involves a "fundamental right," the "compelling interest test" must be applied, which requires the state to prove its particular regulation imposed on home education is "necessary" and the "least restrictive means" to fulfill its interest that children be literate and self-sufficient. This test is described in detail in Chapter 4.

In conclusion, this right of parents to educate their children is a fundamental right along with their right to have their children educated free from government standardization. These two fundamental rights of the parent are protected through the U.S. Supreme Court decisions of *Meyer* and *Pierce*. The liberty to exercise these rights is inseparably connected to the parents' right to control the *process* of education. The states' attempts to arbitrarily regulate and limit parental control of the process of education results in the infringement of the fundamental rights of the parents as designated above.

---

13. *Wisconsin* v. *Yoder*, 406 U.S. at 221 and *Plyler* v. *Doe*, 457 U.S. 202, 221 (1982).

United States Supreme Court Cases Protecting Parents' Rights

In *Meyer* v. *Nebraska*,[14] the Court invalidated a State prohibiting foreign language instruction to school children because the law did not "promote" education but rather "arbitrarily and unreasonably" interfered with "the natural duty of the parent to give his children education suitable to their station in life..."[15] The court chastened the legislature for attempting "materially to interfere... with the power of parents to control the education of their own."[16] This decision clearly affirmed that the Constitution protected the preferences of the parent in education over those of the State.[17] In the same decision, the Supreme Court also recognized that the right of the parents to delegate their authority to a teacher in order to instruct their children was protected within the liberty of the First Amendment.[18]

Furthermore, the Court emphasized, "The Fourteenth Amendment guarantees the right of the individual... to establish a home and bring up children, to worship God according to his own conscience."[19]

In 1925 the Supreme Court decided the *Pierce* v. *Society of Sisters*[20] case, supporting *Meyer's* recognition of the parents' right to direct the religious upbringing of their children and to control the process of their education. In *Pierce*, the Supreme Court struck down an Oregon compulsory education law which, in effect, required attendance of all children between ages eight and sixteen at *public* schools. The Court declared,

---

14. 262 U.S. 390 (1923).

15. *Id.,* at 402.

16. *Id.,* at 401. Also see *Bartles* v. *Iowa*, 262 U.S. 404 (1923) where the Court reached a similar conclusion.

17. Whitehead, John, *Journal of Christian Jurisprudence*, Oklahoma City, Oklahoma: IED Press Inc., 1982, p. 63.

18. *Meyer*, 262 U.S. 390 at 400.

19. *Id.,* at 403.

20. *Pierce*, 268 U.S. 510 (1925).

Under the doctrine of *Meyer v. Nebraska*, we think it entirely plain that the Act of 1922 unreasonably interferes with the liberty of parents and guardians to direct the upbringing and education of children.[21]

In addition to upholding the right of parents to direct or control the education of their children, *Pierce* also asserts the parents' fundamental right to keep their children free from government standardization.

The fundamental theory of liberty upon which all governments in this Union repose excluded any general power of the state to standardize its children by forcing them to accept instruction from public teachers only. *The child is not the mere creature of the state; those who nurture him and direct his destiny have the right and the high duty, to recognize and prepare him for additional obligations.*[22]

The Supreme court uses strong language to assert that children are *not* "the mere creature of the State." The holding in *Pierce*, therefore, preserves diversity of process of education, forbidding the State to standardize the education of children by forcing them to accept instruction only from public schools.

In *Farrington v. Tokushige*, the Court again upheld parental liberty by striking down an act which the Court admits would have destroyed most, if not all private schools.[23] The Court noted that the parent has the right to direct the education of his own child without unreasonable restrictions.[24] In support of this assertion the Court explained,

the capacity to impart instruction to others is given by the Almighty for beneficent purposes and its use may not be forbidden or interfered with by government—certainly

---

21. *Ibid.*, at 534.
22. *Pierce*, 268 U.S. 510 at 535.
23. *Farrington v. Tokushige*, 273 U.S. 284 (1927) at 298.
24. *Id.*, at 298.

not, unless such instruction is, in its nature, harmful to the public morals or imperils the public safety.[25]

The parents' right to instruct their children clearly takes precedence over the States' regulatory interest *unless* public safety is endangered. Similarly, in *Prince v. Massachusetts*,[26] the Supreme Court admitted the high responsibility and right of parents to control the upbringing of their children against that of the State.

> It is cardinal with us that the custody, care, and nurture of the child reside *first* in the *parents*, whose primary function and freedom include preparation for obligations the State can neither supply nor *hinder*.[27] (emphasis supplied)

Twenty-one years later, the Supreme Court in *Griswold v. Connecticut* emphasized that the State cannot interfere with the right of a parent to control his child's education.[28] The Court stated that the right to educate one's child as one chooses, is guaranteed in the Bill of Rights and applicable to the States by the First and Fourteenth Amendments.[29]

Forty-eight years after *Pierce*, the U.S. Supreme Court once again upheld *Pierce* as "the charter of the rights of parents to direct the religious upbringing of their children."[30] In agreement with *Pierce*, Chief Justice Burger stated in the opinion of *Wisconsin v. Yoder* in 1972:

> this case involves the *fundamental interest* of parents, as contrasted with that of the state, to guide the religious future and education of their children. The history and culture of Western civilization reflect a strong tradition of parental

25. *Farrington v. Tokushige*, (9 cir.) 11 F.2d 710 at 713 (1926), quoting Harlan, J., in *Berea College v. Kentucky* 211 U.S. 45, 29 S. Ct. 33, 53 L. Ed. 81.
26. *Prince v. Massachusetts*, 321 U.S. 158 (1944).
27. *Ibid.*, at 166.
28. *Griswold v. Connecticut*, 381 U.S. 479, (1965) at 486.
29. *Ibid.* See Chapter 4 of this book to see the First Amendment basis for parental liberty through the right of parents to freely exercise their religious beliefs.
30. *Yoder*, 406 U.S. 205 a 233.

concern for the nurture and upbringing of their children. This *primary* role of the parents in the upbringing of their children is now established *beyond debate* as an *enduring tradition*.[31] (emphasis supplied)

This case involved an Amish family who wanted their children to be exempt after eighth grade from the public schools and to be instructed at home. Furthermore in *Yoder*, the U.S. Supreme Court emphasized that:

> Thus a state's interest in universal education, however highly we rank it, is not totally free from a balancing process when it impinges on *fundamental* rights and interests, such as those specifically protected by the Free Exercise Clause of the First Amendment, and the traditional interest of parents with respect to the religious upbringing of their children... This case involves the fundamental and religious future and education of their children.[32]

Another decision which upholds the right of parents is *Employment Division of Oregon v. Smith*,[33] which involved two Indians who were fired from a private drug rehabilitation organization because they ingested "peyote," a hallucinogenic drug as part of their religious belief. When they sought unemployment compensation, they were denied because they were discharged for "misconduct."

The Indians appealed to the Oregon Court of Appeals who reversed on the grounds that they had the right to freely exercise their religious beliefs by taking drugs. Of course, as expected, the U.S. Supreme Court reversed the case and found that the First

---

31. *Ibid.,* at 232. Burger admonishes further, "and when the interests of parenthood are combined with a free exercise claim of the nature revealed by this record, **more** than merely a "reasonable relation to some purpose within the competency of the State" is required to sustain the validity of the State's requirement under the First Amendment." (*Yoder*, at 233).

32. *Id.*, at 214.

33. *Smith*, 494 U.S. 872 (1990).

Amendment did not protect harmful drug use. So what does the case have to do with parental rights?

After the Court ruled against the Indians, it then analyzed the application of the Free Exercise Clause generally. The Court wrongly decided to throw out the Free Exercise Clause as a defense to any "neutral" law that might violate an individual's religious convictions. In the process of destroying religious freedom, the Court went out of its way to say that the parents' rights to control the education of their children is still a fundamental right. The Court declared that the "compelling interest test" is still applicable, not to the Free Exercise Clause alone:

> ...but the Free Exercise Clause in conjunction with other **constitutional protections** such as...the **right of parents**, acknowledged in *Pierce* v. *Society of Sisters*, 268 U.S. 510 (1925), **to direct the education of their children**, see *Wisconsin* v. *Yoder*, 406 U.S.205 (1972) invalidating compulsory-attendance laws as applied to Amish parents who refused on religious grounds to send their children to school.[34]

In other words, under this precedent, the fact that a family is home schooling for religious reasons is not enough to be a defense against a state requirement such as teacher certification. However, since that religious conviction to home school is **combined** with the fundamental right of parents to control the education of their children as guaranteed under the Fourteenth Amendment, the home school family battling the restrictive state regulation still is protected by the "compelling interest test." This means the state must prove, with evidence, that teacher certification is necessary for children to be educated and the least restrictive means. The Court in *Smith* quoted its previous case of *Wisconsin* v. *Yoder*:

> *Yoder* said that "The Court's holding in *Pierce* stands as a charter for the rights of parents to direct the religious

---

34. *Id.*, 881.

upbringing of their children. And when the interests of parenthood are combined with a free exercise claim... **more than merely a reasonable relationship** to some purpose within the competency of the State is required to sustain the validity of the State's requirement under the First Amendment." 406 U.S., at 233.[35]

Instead of merely showing that teacher certification is reasonable, the state must, therefore, reach the higher standard of the "compelling interest test" which requires the state to prove teacher certification is the least restrictive means.

On June 5, 2000, one of these most significant U.S. Supreme Court decisions, *Troxel v. Granville*, affirmed parental liberty as a fundamental right. This textbook case on parents' rights is analyzed in Appendix VI.

It is not unusual for the U.S. Supreme Court to apply the "compelling interest test" to all fundamental rights such as parental liberty. The Court has regularly applied this test to fundamental rights that arise out of the Liberty Clause of the Fourteenth Amendment. In *Roe* v. *Wade*, the Court said:

> "Where fundamental rights are involved... regulation limiting these rights may be justified *only* by a *compelling state interest*..."[36]

The compelling interest test and its application are described in detail in Chapter 4.

Parents Are Presumed to Be Acting in Their Child's Best Interest

The United States Supreme Court, in *Parham* v. *J.R.*,[37] presented strong support of parents' rights to control the important

---

35. *Id.,* 881, ftn. 1.
36. *Roe* v. *Wade*, 410 U.S. 113, 155 (1973).

decisions which concern their minor children. In that case, Chief Justice Burger wrote for the majority:

> Our jurisprudence historically has reflected Western civilization concepts of the family as a unit with broad parental authority over minor children. Our cases have consistently followed that course; our constitutional system long ago rejected any notion that a child is "the mere creature of the State" and, on the contrary, asserted that parents generally "have the right, coupled with the high duty, to recognize and prepare [their children] for additional obligations." *Pierce* v. *Society of Sisters*, 268 U.S. 510, 535 (1925)... [other citations omitted]... The law's concept of the family rests on a presumption that parents possess what a child lacks in maturity, experience, and capacity for judgment required for making life's difficult decisions. More important, historically it has been recognized that natural bonds of affection lead parents to act in the best interests of their children. 1 W. Blackstone, Commentaries 447; 2 J. Kent, Commentaries on American Law 190.
>
> As with so many other legal presumptions, experience and reality may rebut what the law accepts as a starting point; the incidence of child neglect and abuse cases attests to this. That some parents "may at times be acting against the interests of their children"... creates a basis for caution, but it is hardly a reason to discard wholesale those pages of human experience that teach that parents generally do act in the child's best interest... The statist notion that governmental power should supercede parental authority in *all* cases because *some* parents abuse and neglect children is repugnant to American tradition.
> ...
> We cannot assume that the result in *Meyer* v. *Nebraska* and *Pierce* v. *Society of Sisters* would have been different if the children there had announced a preference to learn only

---

37. *Parham*, 442 U.S. 584 (1979).

English or a preference to go to a public, rather than a church school.[38]

The U.S. Supreme Court is recognizing that there is a presumption that parents act in the best interests of their children. This includes the area of education. This is a heavy burden the state must overcome in order to regulate how parents must educate their children. "The statist notion that governmental power should supercede parental authority in all cases because some parents abuse and neglect children is repugnant to American tradition."

Similarly in 1909, the Oklahoma Supreme Court ruled on a landmark case, *School Board Dist. No 18* v. *Thompson*,[39] which secured the right of parents to control the education of their children, even though the Oklahoma constitution and Legislature recently enacted compulsory education. In this case, parents of children in the public school did not want their children to receive singing lessons, so the public school expelled them. The parents tried to get their children reinstated in the public schools, and this case resulted.

The attorney representing the school district contended that "the old common-law idea that the parent has the exclusive control over the education of the child has long since been abandoned" since the state requirement of compulsory education was enacted.[40] The Oklahoma Supreme Court, however, unanimously disagreed with the school district and ruled:

> A better rule, we think, would be to presume . . . that the request of the parent (to exempt child from singing lessons) was reasonable and just, to the best interest of the child . . .
> The parent . . . has a right to make a reasonable selection from the prescribed course of study for his child to pursue, and this selection must be respected by the school author-

---

38. *Parham*, 442 U.S., at 602-604.
39. *Thompson*, 103 P. 578, 24 L.R.A. 221, 24 Okla. 1.
40. *Thompson*, 24 Okla. at 4.

ities, *as the right of the parent in that regard is superior to that of the school officers and the teachers.*[41]

In other words, the Court found that the parents' right to control the education of their children supersedes the state's authority under compulsory education laws even when the child is in the public schools. The Court explained further:

> Under our form of government, and at common law, *the home* is considered the keystone of the governmental structure. In this empire, *parents rule supreme* during the minority of their children.[42]

The Court also quoted Blackstone as strong support for their decision to uphold parents' rights to control their child's education:

> Blackstone says that the greatest duty of parents to their children is that of giving them an education suitable to their station in life; a duty pointed out by reason, and of far the greatest importance of any. But this duty at common law was not compulsory; the common law presuming that the natural love and affection of the parents for their children would impel them to faithfully perform this duty, and deeming it punishment enough to leave the parent, who neglects the instruction of his family, to labor under those griefs and inconveniences which his family, so uninstructed, will be sure to bring upon him. Lewis' Blackstone, book 1, §451.[43]

Building upon these parental right principles of common law, the Court concluded that the Oklahoma law modifies that absolute parental right very minimally. The parents' rights are still supreme since the public school's authority is given by the parents and limited by the parents.

---

41. *Thompson*, at 11.
42. *Thompson*, at 9.
43. *Thompson*, at 8.

State and Federal Cases Recognizing the Fundamental Right of Parents to Educate Their Children

In *Ohio v. Whisner*, the Tabernacle Christian School refused to follow Ohio's minimum standards for all schools and asserted that the regulations unconstitutionally interfered with their right to freely exercise their professed beliefs.[44] The Supreme Court of Ohio held,

> In our view, these [minimum] standards are so pervasive and all-encompassing that total compliance with each and every standard by a non-public school would effectively eradicate the distinction between public and non-public education, and thereby deprive these appellants of their traditional interest as parents to direct the upbringing and education of their children.
>
> ... And equally difficult to imagine is a state interest sufficiently substantial to sanction abrogation of appellants'[parents] liberty to direct the education of their children. We will not, therefore, attempt to conjure up such an interest...[45]

The Court, therefore, exempted Christian schools from these minimum standards which dictated curriculum content, manner of socialization, quality of teaching, and parental involvement in education. Standardization and regimentation in the field of learning is contrary to the American concept of individual liberty.[46]

The Ohio Supreme Court , in *Whisner*, concluded:

> Thus, it has long been recognized that the right of a parent to guide the education, including the religious educa-

---

44. *Ohio v. Whisner*, 351 N.E. 2d 750 (1976) at 761.
45. *Ibid.,* at 768
46. *North Carolina v. Williams* 117 S.E. 2d 444 (1960) at 450.

tion, of his or her children is indeed a fundamental right guaranteed under the Fourteenth Amendment.[47]

In *Windsor Park Baptist Church v. Arkansas Activities Association* the U.S. Court of Appeals cautioned the State of Arkansas not to standardize its children by forcing them to accept instruction from public teachers only. The Court states,

> The Fourteenth Amendment forbids the States to prohibit attendance at nonpublic schools, either secular or religious.[48]

In other words, the State must be careful not to overly regulate home schools and Christian schools to the extent they cannot operate, thereby forcing their children to attend only public schools.

Several other courts have recognized that the fundamental right of parents recognized in *Pierce* is applicable to home schooling situations. The Massachusetts Supreme Judicial Court in *Care and Protection of Charles*, ruled in favor of the home schooling family, stating that home education is a "right protected by the Fourteenth Amendment."[49] The Court further stated that the object of the compulsory attendance laws is "that all children shall be educated, not that they shall be educated in any particular way."[50]

In Pennsylvania, a Federal Court ruled on the side of parents rights in the *Jeffery v. O'Donnell* case, involving home schoolers, because it recognized that "parents have a substantial constitutional right to direct and control the upbringing and development of their minor children."[51] Similarly, in Indiana, another Federal Court in the *Mazanec* case ruled that parents have a "constitutional right to educate their children in a home environment."[52]

---

47. *Whisner*, at 769.
48. *Windsor Park Baptist Church v. Arkansas Activities Association*, (658 F 2d 618 [1981] at 621).
49. *Charles*, 504 N.E.2d 592, 598 (Mass. 1987).
50. *Id.*, at 600.
51. *Jeffery v. O'Donnell I.*, 702 F. Supp. 513, 515 (1988).
52. *Mazanec v. North Judson-San Pierre School Corporation*, 614 F. Supp. 1152, 1160 (N.D. Ind. 1985).

In *Appeal of Pierce,*[53] the New Hampshire Supreme Court ruled in favor of a home schooling family who had been denied their right to home school without due process by the State Board of Education. In a concurring opinion two justices asserted,

> This court specifically cited this quotation [from *Yoder*] in reaffirming the *fundamental rights* of parents to the custody, care and nurture of their children. *State* v. *Robert H.*, 118 N.H. 713, 715, 339 A2d. 1387, 1388 (1978). Indeed at common law the parents' authority over the education of their children was unquestionably a natural right which arose out of those parental responsibilities. See 1 W. Blackstone, Commentaries 450-53 (1809); *People* v. *Stanley*, 81 Colo 276, 280-81, 255 P. 610, 613 (1927). Thus, while the State may adopt a policy requiring children to be educated, it does not have the unlimited power to require they be educated in a certain way at a certain place. N. Edwards, *The Courts and the Public Schools*, at 521 (1971).
> Home education is an enduring American tradition and right... Thus approval requirements for non-public school education may not unnecessarily interfere with traditional parental rights.

The New Hampshire Supreme Court clearly recognized that parents right to home schooling is a fundamental right, and that right is to be free from standardization.

Lastly, a Federal Court in Missouri in the *Ellis* case ruled in favor of the home schoolers and applied "stringent scrutiny" because the case involved "the constitutional right of parents to direct the upbringing of their children and inculcate religious and educational values in their offspring."[54] This case resulted in the best home school law in the country, providing maximum freedom for home schoolers.

---

53. *Appeal of Pierce* 451 A.2d 363, 367 (NH, 1982).
54. *Ellis* v. *O'Hara*, 612 F.Supp. 379 (E.D.Mo. 1985) [reversed on mootness grounds].

Fundamental Right Against Standardization of Education

Oftentimes standardization of home schools by requiring them to be "approved" by public school authorities creates nothing more than "mini-public schools in the home." Making the regulations so severe as to eradicate the distinction between home and public education is to destroy the alternative of private education guaranteed by *Pierce*. In addition, such standardization would inhibit the invaluable contributions of private and home education in promoting high academics and high morals.[55] Such regulations also deny the historic and fundamental right of parents to have their children free from standardization of their education.

The use of public schools to instill political and religious values uniformly throughout all schools poses a serious threat to the marketplace of ideas and the integrity of the democratic process.[56] Regulations conforming all schools, including home schools, to the teaching standards, curriculum content, and social levels of public schools destroys diversity and creates a danger of "despotism over the mind".[57]

---

55. *Williams, supra.* The Supreme Court of North Carolina comments,
   It would be difficult to over-estimate the contribution of private institutions of learning to the initiative, progress, and individualism of our people. Regulation should *never* be resorted to unless the need is compellingly apparent.
See Chapter 1 of this book for documentation as to the benefits of home schooling.
   56. Kamenshine, 67 Colo. L. Rev. 1104 at 1134.
   57. John Stuart Mill, who wrote the famous book *On Liberty*, in the early 1700s, greatly influenced the framers of the U.S. Constitution regarding the limited role of government in the economy and education. Mill cautioned governments in his book stating,
   A general State education is a *mere contrivance* for *molding people* to be *exactly* like one *another*: and as the mould in which it casts them is that which pleases the predominant power in the government or [the will of] the majority of the existing generations; in proportion as it is efficient and successful, it establishes a *despotism* over the *mind*, leading by natural tendency to one over the body.

In Germany in 1933, for example, Hitler rose to power while simultaneously gaining control of the State-controlled educational system. In 1936, Hitler abolished all Christian schools in Germany, forcing all children to be enrolled in public school in order to indoctrinate them in fascism.[58] Two years later, he ordered all public school teachers to resign from all denominations.[59]

The lesson to be learned, therefore, is that it is necessary to preserve diversity in education in order to prevent the potential abuses of a totally state-controlled educational system. For home schoolers, the less governmental control the better. The Supreme Court has consistently upheld this fundamental right of parents to have their children free from standardization in a long line of cases.

Although *Meyer*, *Pierce*, *Farrington*, *Yoder*, *Jeffery*, *Whisner*, and many other cases uphold the parental right to control the process of their child's education and to be educated free from state standardization, a number of past state cases have derived certain language from *Meyer*, *Pierce*, and *Yoder* to cause an expansion of the State's control over private education. These latter cases, *Shaver* (ND), *Patzer* (ND), *Faith Baptist* (NE), *Fellowship Baptist* (IA), *McDonough* (ME), *Riddle* (WV) and *Sheridan Road Baptist* (MI) have used the State's compelling interest in education as an excuse to regulate all private, Christian schools into conformity with public school standards. They, however, have not applied or have mis-

---

(emphasis supplied)

(Benton, William, Publisher, *American State Papers: On Liberty by John Stuart Mill*, Chicago: Encyclopedia, Inc., 1972, p. 318.

58. Koch, H,W. *Hitler Youth: The Duped Generation*, New York: Ballantine Books, 1972, p. 104.

Historian William Shirer similarly documents the legal measures the German government used to coerce those parents who refused to send their child to public school. Criminal prosecutions were applied to such parents.

"Recalcitrant parents were warned that their children would be taken away from them and put in orphanages or other homes unless they enrolled." (See Shirer, William, *The Rise and Fall of the Third Reich*, New York: Simon and Schuster, 1060, p. 255).

59. Koch, at 104.

applied the high standard of the mandatory "compelling interest test" as discussed in detail in Chapter 5. Instead, these courts have applied the lesser standard of "reasonableness."

Fortunately, these cases, attempting to increase State control, have *all* been rendered moot or ineffective by the state legislatures simply changing the laws to protect parents' rights to home school or by a higher court, as is the case in Michigan.

State Parental Rights Acts as Amendments

Like other fundamental constitutional rights, the right of parents to direct their children's education should only be overcome by the state upon satisfying the stringent burdens of proof required in the "compelling interest test." This, of course, is the exact same showing that the state must make under the Free Exercise Clause analysis as discussed in the next chapter and it is a much higher standard than showing mere "reasonableness."

Many other states, faced with similar court decisions denying parental rights as fundamental, have sought to enact parental rights acts or state constitutional amendments. Appendix II provides a thorough look at the state trends in this area. It also includes model parental rights language already enacted or to be enacted by state legislatures in order to stop the courts' erosion of parental rights. Many other parental rights decisions are summarized in this appendix demonstrating the need for this corrective action.

4 The Free Exercise of Religion and the Right to Home School

Most home schoolers are home schooling for religious reasons as shown by several recent studies.[1] Many of these families believe they are called by God to be the primary teachers of their children.

Since these families have strong religious beliefs that they must home school, they are protected by the First Amendment of the United States Constitution, which guarantees all citizens the right to freely exercise their religious beliefs. This means that a home school family who is being prosecuted for not complying with a local restriction on their home school — such as the requirement of a college degree or teaching certificate — can use the First Amendment as a defense as long as they prove the particular restriction violates their religious belief.

The Four-Part Compelling Interest Test

Whenever the right of parents to educate their children under either the 1st or 14th Amendment is at issue, a specific legal test

---

1. Dr. Brian Ray, "A Nationwide Study of Home Education," November 16, 1990, National Home Education Research Institute, Seattle, WA. This study of over 2000 home school families found that 93.8 percent of the fathers and 96.4 percent of the mothers describe themselves as "born-again" Christians.

49

must be applied. This test is made up of four parts and it is often referred to as the "compelling interest test."[2]

The U.S. Supreme Court has stated that whenever parental rights are combined with a free exercise claim, a heightened standard of review must be applied.[3] This standard of review involves the application of the "compelling interest" test which requires the home schooler asserting a religious belief to prove two parts of the test and requiring the State to prove the other two parts. This test was originally applied in *Sherbert* v. *Verner*,[4] and has evolved through the years in *Wisconsin* v. *Yoder*,[5] *Thomas* v. *Review Board*,[6] *U.S.* v. *Lee*,[7] and *Hobbie* v. *Unemployment Appeals Comm'n of Florida*.[8] This test involves *four* major parts.

First of all, the burden is on the home school family to prove the first two parts of the "compelling interest" test: (1) They must demonstrate that their religious belief against the particular state requirement is both "sincere" and "religious;"[9] (2) secondly, the home school family must prove that their sincere religious belief is "burdened" *as applied* under the facts.[10]

Then the burden shifts to the state to prove, with evidence, the last two parts of test. The two burdens the state must prove are that its requirement is "essential" or "necessary" "to accomplish an over-riding governmental [or compelling] interest" in education,[11] and that "it is the least restrictive means of achieving some compelling state interest."[12] If the state can prove its interest in a particular reg-

---

2. See *Wisconsin* v. *Yoder*, 406 U.S.205, (1972) and *Sherbert* v. *Verner*, 374 U.S. 398, (1963).

3. *Yoder*, 406 U.S. 205, 233 (1972).

4. *Sherbert*, 374 U.S. 398 (1963).

5. *Yoder*, 406 U.S. 205 (1972).

6. *Thomas*, 450 U.S. 707 (1981).

7. *Lee*, 455 U.S. 252, (1982).

8. *Hobbie*, 480 U.S. 136, 94 L.Ed.2d 190, 197-198 (1987).

9. *Yoder*, 406 U.S. at 216-219.

10. *Yoder*, 406 U.S. at 215-219; *Thomas*, 450 U.S. at 713-716.

11. *Lee*, *supra*, 455 U.S. at 257.

12. *Thomas*, *supra*, 450 U.S. at 718.

ulation is necessary and the least restrictive means, then the religious belief of the home schooler must give way. What is the state's legitimate interest in education? According to U.S. Supreme Court precedent, the state's interest is two-fold: **civic and economic**.[13] The state has an interest that children will acquire the necessary reading and writing skills to be able to vote and participate in our democratic system. The second interest of the state is that children will be able to eventually provide for themselves so that they will not become a burden on the state's welfare rolls. Many courts are finding that some of the present compulsory attendance laws are overly restrictive concerning home schools.

For example, a state requiring a college degree for home school parents would fail the third part of the "compelling interest test" since a college degree is not "essential" or "necessary" for a child to be educated. As seen in Chapter 10, all available studies prove there is no positive correlation between teacher qualifications and student performance.

Furthermore, a state like North Dakota, which requires home school parents to take a teacher's exam, is not using the least restrictive means to achieve the state's civil and economic interest. Forty-nine other states do not require such a standard of teacher qualifications, demonstrating that the requirement of a teacher's exam is not the least restrictive means.

First Step: Are the Home School Family's Beliefs Sincere and Religious?

As stated above, the first step in free exercise analysis is to examine whether the religious beliefs in question are both "sin-

---

13. *Yoder, supra*, at 221, *Plyler* v. *Doe*, 457 U.S. 202, 221 (1982) and *New Life Baptist Church* v. *Town of East Longmeadow*, 666 F.Supp. 293 (D.Mass. 1987) at 317-318.

cere" and "religious."[14] The truth of the belief is not open to question;[15] rather, the issue is whether that belief is "truly-held."[16]

Parents who home school their children for religious reasons are often opposed on the same religious grounds to various restrictions placed on them by the state. The First Amendment guarantees these families the right to freely exercise their religious beliefs and thus be exempted from the state requirements.

Parents, however, must provide proof in two areas if they use the Free Exercise Defense in court: (1) they must prove that their beliefs are religious, and (2) they must prove their religious beliefs are "sincerely-held." This is particularly important for home schoolers in states like Virginia, where there are statutory religious exemptions from compulsory attendance which can only be obtained by proving to the school board that they have bona fide religious beliefs concerning their children's education.

The United States Supreme Court has set clear standards in these two areas.

The Case Law Defining What Is a Religious Belief

First of all, it is important to analyze the leading case which established the test of determining whether someone's beliefs are religious rather than merely philosophical.

In *Wisconsin v. Yoder*, the Supreme Court discussed which type of beliefs are protected and which are not.

> A way of life, however virtuous and admirable, may not be interposed as a barrier to reasonable state regulation of education if it is based on purely secular considerations; to have the protection of the Religion Clauses, the claims

---

14. *Wisconsin v. Yoder*, 406 U.S. 205, 216-219 (1972).
15. *United States v. Ballard*, 322 U.S. 78, 87 (1944).
16. *United States v. Seeger*, 380 U.S. 163, 185 (1965).

must be rooted in religious belief . . . Thus, if the Amish asserted their claims because of their subjective evaluation and rejection of the contemporary secular values accepted by the majority, much as Thoreau rejected the social values of his time and isolated himself at Walden Pond, their claims would not rest on a religious base. Thoreau's choice was philosophical and personal rather than religious, and such belief does not rise to the demands of the Religion Clauses.[17]

Beliefs which are *"philosophical **and** personal"* are not entitled to Free Exercise protection.

The U.S. Supreme Court in 1965, in the case *U.S.* v. *Seeger*[18], defined "religious training and belief" as a "sincere and meaningful belief which occupies in the life of its possessor a place parallel to that filled by God."[19] The Court further declared,

Within that phrase would come all sincere religious beliefs which are based upon a power or being, or upon a faith, to which all else is subordinate or upon which all else is ultimately dependent.[20]

The Court also explained that a belief is not religious if it is essentially political, sociological, or philosophical or based merely on a personal moral code. The Court explained that "merely personal" refers to "a moral code which is not only personal but which is the *sole* basis for the registrant's belief *and is no way related to a Supreme Being.*" From this definition of the term "religious" by the U.S. Supreme Court, a particular family's beliefs are, in fact, *religious* if their entire belief system is dependent on a supernatural God and His revelation.

---

17. *Yoder*, 406 U.S. 205, at 215-16.
18. *Seeger*, 380 U.S. 163, 13 L.Ed. 2d 733, 85 S.Ct. 850 (1965).
19. *Seeger*, 380 U.S. 176.
20. *Id.*, at 176.

The Case Law Defining a Sincerely-Held Religious Belief

The U.S. Supreme Court has offered some guidelines on determining whether an individual's religious beliefs are sincere. In *Thomas* v. *Review Board*,[21] the Court stated "religious beliefs need not be acceptable, logical, consistent, or comprehensible to others in order to merit First Amendment protection."[22] Furthermore, in *U.S.* v. *Ballard*,[23] the Court declared "in applying the Free Exercise Clause, courts may not inquire into the truth, validity, or reasonableness of a claimant's religious beliefs."

Also according to the U.S. Supreme Court in *Hobbie*, the timing of one's religious beliefs are irrelevant and "immaterial."

So long as one's faith is *religiously-based* at the time it is asserted, it should not matter, for constitutional purposes, whether that faith is derived from revelation, study, upbringing, gradual evolution, or some source that appears entirely incomprehensible.[24]

It is important to emphasize that the First Amendment also protects personal religious convictions which are *not* held by all members of the particular religious sect with which the person is a member. The Court in the *Thomas* case ruled that they must "allow for intrafaith differences" because:

the guarantee of free exercise is not limited to beliefs which are shared by all of the members of a religious sect. Particularly in this sensitive area, it is not within the judicial function and judicial competence to inquire whether the petitioner or his fellow worker more correctly perceived

---

21. *Thomas,* 450 U.S. 707, (1980).
22. *Id.,* at 714.
23. *Ballard,* 322 U.S. 78 (1944).
24. *Hobbie* v. *Unemployment Appeals Commission,* 480 U.S. 136, 94 L.Ed 2d 190, 199 (1987).

the commands of their common faith. Courts are not arbiters of scriptural interpretation.[25]

The U.S. Supreme Court realized that "Thomas drew a line" concerning what he believed, and they had no right to question it. The commonly raised issue of whether a family's religious conviction concerning home schooling must be supported by a tenet or church doctrine of their church or denomination in order for them to be entitled to a religious exemption has also clearly been settled by the U.S. Supreme Court. The case, *Frazee* v. *Illinois Department of Employment Security*,[26] held that in order for a religious belief to be legitimate or bona fide, the religious belief may be personal and *not* mandated by a church.

The Court ruled that whether or not the individual's church "formally" supports the religious belief held by the individual is "an irrelevant issue" in determining the legitimacy of that religious belief.[27]

The case involved a man (Frazee) who, although not part of any particular church or denomination, claimed he was a Christian and that his religious convictions prohibited him from working on Sunday. He refused a job that would have required him to work on Sunday. When he applied for unemployment, his application was denied because the Illinois agency had a policy which would not recognize *personal religious beliefs* but only religious beliefs that are based on some tenet of a church or denomination. The U.S. Supreme Court finally ruled that Frazee's personal beliefs are legitimate and protected by the First Amendment. As a result, Frazee can collect unemployment. The Court held:

> Undoubtedly, membership in an organized religious denomination, especially one with a specific tenet forbidding

---

25. *Thomas* v. *Review Board*, 450 U.S. 707, 715-716 (1981).
26. *Frazee*, 489 US, 103 L.Ed 2d 914, (March 29, 1989).
27. *Id.*, 103 L.Ed 2d at 919.

members to work on Sunday, would simplify the problem of identifying sincerely held religious beliefs, **but we reject the notion that to claim the protection of the Free Exercise clause, one must be responding to the commands of a particular religious organization.**[28]

In other words, the Court is emphasizing that a person's religious beliefs can be "sincere" and legitimate even though they are not supported by any particular church tenet. *Personal* religious beliefs are bona fide and are protected by the First Amendment of the U.S. Constitution.

Regarding several of its earlier cases on this subject of sincerity of religious convictions, the Court stated:

> It is true, as the Illinois court noted, that each of the claimants in those cases was a member of a particular religious sect, but none of those decisions turned on that consideration or on any tenet of the sect involved that forbade the work the claimant refused to perform. Our judgments in those cases rested on the fact that each of the claimants had a *sincere belief* that religion required him or her to refrain from the work in question. *Never did we suggest* that unless a claimant belongs to a sect that forbids what his job requires, his belief, however sincere, must be deemed a purely personal preference rather than a religious beliefs.[29]

Conclusion: the True Criteria

The *only true criteria*, therefore, a court should apply when considering whether a family's religious beliefs are sincere is whether or not the particular family has demonstrated through their lifestyle that they perceive God as being a life-controlling, conduct-regu-

---

28. *Frazee,* 103 L.Ed 2d at 920.
29. *Frazee*, 103 L.Ed 2d at 919.

lating force in their lives. In all respects, their religious beliefs must be "inseparable and interdependent." This is the only true "litmus test" a particular family needs to pass in order to be determined as having "sincere" beliefs.[30]

Step Two: Are the Home Schoolers' Religious Beliefs Burdened?

The second step for the home schooler is to prove that their religious belief concerning home schooling their children is being burdened or violated by the state's requirement. This is fairly easy to prove. For instance, if the state requires the home schooler to submit their curriculum to the local school district for approval in violation of their religious beliefs and the State then takes action to enforce its view by subjecting these parents to criminal prosecution, conviction, and sentencing for acting in accordance with their religious beliefs, that family can prove a burden.

In *Wisconsin v. Yoder*, Jonas Yoder was prosecuted for truancy for keeping his children at home in obedience to his sincerely held religious beliefs. In that case, the United States Supreme Court emphasized the fact that when a person is criminally prosecuted for taking action in accordance with his or her religious beliefs that is proof of a "burden" thus satisfying the second part of the test. In *Lyng v. Northwest Indian Cemetery Protective Association*,[31] the Court said:

> The statute at issue in that case [*Yoder*] prohibited the Amish parents, on pain of criminal prosecution, from providing their children with the kind of education required by the Amish religion... The statute directly compelled the Amish

---

30. See *Wisconsin v. Yoder*, 406 U.S. 205, 215 (1972).
31. *Lyng*, 485 U.S. 439, 108 S.Ct. 1319, 1329, 99 L.Ed. 2d 534 (1988).

to send their children to public high schools 'contrary to the Amish religion and way of life.'

When a state requirement directly conflicts with a person's religious belief a "burden," or constitutional coercion, has been shown.

Step Three: The State Must Prove Its Requirement Is Essential

The United States Supreme Court has made it clear that the state, not the parents, has the burden of proving that its particular regulation, which is in conflict with the home schooler's religious beliefs, is "essential" for children to be educated. In the *Hobbie* case the Court said: "Both *Sherbert* and *Thomas* held that such infringements must be subjected to strict scrutiny and could be justified only by proof by the State of a compelling interest." [32] It is not the burden of the parents to prove this. If the state can not prove its regulation is essential, the family's religious beliefs will be protected. The State cannot prevail on the compelling interest test if it introduces no evidence to support its position. In *Carey* v. *Population Services International,*[33] the Supreme Court held that the state cannot prevail when "there is a conceded absence of supporting evidence" to support a claim of the power to override a fundamental freedom.

The Supreme Court has made it clear in *U.S.* v. *Lee* that as a part of the compelling interest test there must be a showing of the "essentiality" of the particular requirement.

> The state may justify a limitation on religious liberty by showing that it is *essential* to accomplish an overriding governmental interest...[34]

---

32. *Hobbie* v. *Unemployment Appeals Comm'n of Florida*, 480 U.S. 136, 141 (1987).
33. *Carey,* 431 U.S. 678, 696 (1977).
34. *United States* v. *Lee*, 455 U.S. 252, 257 (1982).

Furthermore, in *Widmar* v. *Vincent*,[35] the United States Supreme Court emphasized that the state "must show that its regulation is *necessary* to serve a compelling state interest..." Michigan Supreme Court Justice Riley in her dissent in *Sheridan Road II* (with Justices Levin and Cavanagh concurring) acknowledged the "compelling interest test," when properly applied, demands the state to prove its regulation is essential:

> The individual religious autonomy guaranteed by the First Amendment's Free Exercise Clause is not absolute, and the state may justify enforcing the regulation notwithstanding the interference with plaintiffs' religious freedom by showing that enforcement is *essential* to the fulfillment of a compelling state interest.
>
> ...
>
> In order to justify averring plaintiffs' fundamental First and Fourteenth rights, the state must establish that enforcing the certification requirement, without exception, is *essential* to ensure the adequate "secular" education required by the compulsory attendance law.[36]

This reasoning was finally affirmed by a majority of the Michigan Supreme Court in *DeJonge* as explained below.

In short, there must be proof that the requirement is both "essential" and "necessary" to achieve the state's interest in an adequate education.[37]

---

35. *Widmar*, 454 U.S. 263, 270 (1981).

36. *Sheridan Road*, 396 N.W. 2d 373 (1986) at 416-417.

37. The following U.S. Supreme Court decisions also utilized the term "essential" or "necessary" when describing the compelling interest test:

"The Court of Appeals found the injunction to be content based and neither necessary to serve a compelling interest nor narrowly drawn to achieve that end." — *Madsen v. Women's Health Center*, 512 US __, __, (1994).

"[W]e think it clear that a government regulation is sufficiently justified ... if the incidental restriction on the alleged First Amendment freedom is no greater than is essential to that [governmental] interest." — *Barnes v. Glen Theatre Inc.*, 501 US 560, 567, (1991).

Step Four: The State Must Prove Its Requirement Is the Least Restrictive Means of Fulfilling the State' Interest

The fourth part of the test demands that even if the state could establish that a particular regulation is "compelling," it must still carry an additional burden and "demonstrate," with evidence, that no alternative form of regulation exists which would be less restrictive to the First Amendment rights involved.[38] In *Yoder*, the Supreme Court said that not only must the interest be of the highest order, the interest must not be "otherwise served."[39]

The state's interest in home schooling cases is that the child receive a "basic education" that will achieve the state's two-fold interest in literacy and economic self-sufficiency. The United States Supreme Court held in *Yoder* that Wisconsin's interest in compulsory education was "otherwise served" by the Amish program of informal home training in the practical and occupation skills of living and working given by their parents and community.

Since the Home School Legal Defense Association was founded in 1983, it has not had a single case, out of hundreds of home school cases, where the home schooled children in question were not receiving an adequate education. In every case, the children were literate and average or above average on their standardized achievement test results (see Chapter 1). The "interest" of the state in children being educated was being "otherwise served." In

---

"For the state to enforce a content-based exclusion it must show that its regulation is necessary to serve a compelling state interest and that it is narrowly drawn to achieve that end." — *Perry Ed. Assn. v. Perry Local Ed. Assn.*, 460 US 37, 45, (1983).

"[The] appellees were exercising a constitutional right, and any classification which serves to penalize the exercise of that right, unless shown to be necessary to promote a compelling government interest, is unconstitutional." — *Shapiro v. Thompson*, 394 US 618, 634, (1969).

38. *Sherbert* v. *Verner*, 374 U.S. 398, 407 (1963).

39. *Yoder*, 406 U.S. at 215.

fact, the public schools are the one school system where the interest of the state is often *not* being met.

The "otherwise served" concept is key to the "least restrictive means" burden of the compelling interest test. The U.S. Supreme Court in *Thomas* clarified "the state may justify an inroad on religious liberty by showing that it is the least restrictive means of achieving some compelling state interest.[40] Before the state can trample the religious convictions of American citizens, it carries the burden of proving that there is no other way to accomplish its objective.

Comparison of an excessive requirement in one state to less burdensome home school requirements in other states can be used to demonstrate that the excessive requirement is *not the least restrictive means available* to satisfy a state's interest in seeing that children taught at home receive an adequate education.[41]

Whether or not a state proves its restriction on home school parents is "reasonable" is irrelevant and does not meet the proper standard. The higher standard of the "compelling interest test" must be applied in home school cases. The U.S. Supreme Court in *Yoder* emphasized the necessity of applying this "stricter scrutiny:"

> And when the interests of parenthood are combined with a free exercise claim...more than merely a reasonable relationship to some purpose within competency of the state

---

40. *Thomas*, 450 U.S. 707, 718 (1981). Also see Appendix IV for additional U.S. Supreme Court cites.

41. It is important to note that in reaching a decision on the least restrictive means issue, the United States Supreme Court has often looked to the experience of other states as a part of the evaluation of a claimed compelling state interest. See, e.g., *McDaniel* v. *Paty*, 435 U.S. 618 (1978). Comparison to other states has also been made by the Supreme Court for the purpose of evaluating the least restrictive means tests. See, e.g., *Thomas* v. *Review Board, supra.* ["there is no evidence in the record to indicate that such inquiries will occur in Indiana, *or that they have occurred in any of the states that extend benefits to people in the petitioner's position.*" 450 U.S. at 719]. [Emphasis added.]

is required to sustain the validity of the state's requirement under the First Amendment.[42]

Virtually all regulations on education could be justified as "reasonable," but many cannot be proven "essential." The requirement that fundamental rights must be protected by the higher standard of the "compelling interest test" requires the state to prove its regulation is both "essential" and "the least restrictive means."

For example, a federal district court in *Jeffery v. O'Donnell*[43] struck down a vague compulsory attendance law in Pennsylvania that was being abused by the 501 school districts in the state. Many school districts were disapproving and prosecuting home schoolers based solely upon arbitrary standards created by the whims of biased school superintendents. The federal district court realized since free exercise rights were involved, a stricter scrutiny had to be applied. The court stated:

> ... When First Amendment rights are affected by the enforcement of a statute, the state law will be held to a *higher standard* of specificity than might be the case if purely economic regulation was at issue.
>
> ...
>
> The threat to sensitive First Amendment freedoms mandates judicial intrusion in the form of declaring the particular provision of the law unconstitutional for vagueness.[44]

Michigan Supreme Court Secures Educational and Religious Liberty

One important state supreme court case handled by Home School Legal Defense Association (HSLDA) which applied "strict scrutiny" to protect home schools was *Michigan v. DeJonge*.[45]

---

42. *Yoder*, 406 U.S. at 233.
43. *Jeffery*, 702 F.Supp. 516 (M.D. Pa 1988).
44. *Id.,* at 519 and 521.
45. *De Jonge*, 501 N.W. 2d 127 (Mich. 1993).

The reason that *DeJonge* is so significant is that, in this case, the Michigan Supreme Court properly applied the four-point "compelling interest test" discussed above.

The *DeJonge* case involved a home school family that was teaching their children successfully but were not certified teachers as required by law. Therefore, they were criminally prosecuted and convicted. The first few appellate courts upheld the conviction, but the Michigan Supreme Court reversed it.

In order to satisfy the first part of the "compelling interest test," the DeJonges had to prove that they had a sincere religious belief against being certified or using a certified teacher. Secondly, the family had to prove that their religious beliefs were burdened by the state's requirement. The Michigan Supreme Court found that the DeJonges easily met both parts of the "compelling interest test." The Court stated:

> As noted, the DeJonges believe that the Word of God commands them to educate their children without state certification. Any regulation interfering with that commandment is state regulation of religion. The certification requirement imposes upon the DeJonges a loathsome dilemma: they must either violate the law of God to abide by the law of man or commit a crime under the law of man to remain faithful to God. The requirement presents a irreconcilable conflict between the mandates of law and religious duty...[46]

According to the U.S. Supreme Court, the burden of proof for the second two parts of the "compelling interest test" rests on the prosecution. In the DeJonge's case, the state had to prove that teacher certification was essential for children to be educated, and that it was the least restrictive means of fulfilling their interest in the children's education. The state had never proven these two points. Nonetheless, the Court of Appeals refused to reverse the decision.

---

46. *DeJonge*, at 137.

The Michigan Supreme Court, however, carefully applied the complete "compelling interest test." The Court acknowledges that although education is important,

> ...Our rights are meaningless if they do not permit an individual to challenge and be free from those abridgments of liberty that are otherwise vital to society: 'Freedom of worship is not limited to things that do not matter much. That would be a mere shadow of freedom. The test of its substance is the right to differ as to the things that touch the heart of the existing order.' *West Virginia Bd. of Ed. v. Barnette,* 319 U.S. 624 (1942), 638, 642. Hence, Michigan's interest in compulsory education is not absolute and must yield to the constitutional liberties protected by the First Amendment.[47]

In other words, the Michigan Supreme Court affirmed that religious freedom should not automatically lose in the face of a conflicting state regulation. This decision is refreshing. Many other state supreme courts discussed in Chapter 5 have improperly held that since the individuals' free exercise rights are not absolute, all home school parents always lose and must yield to the states' interests in compulsory education.

Regarding Michigan's compelling interest in teacher certification, the Court found out the state did not prove any compelling interest. The only "compelling interest" the state proved was its interest in education generally. However, the state's interest in education *is* being fulfilled by the DeJonges successfully home schooling their children. The Court ruled:

> Indeed, such a searching examination in the instant case is enlightening because it reveals that the state has focused upon the incorrect governmental interest. The state's interest is not ensuring that the goals of compulsory education are met, because the state does not contest that the DeJonges are succeeding at fulfilling such aims. Rather, the state's

---

47. *Id.,* at 139.

interest is simply the certification requirement... *not* the general objectives of compulsory education. The interest the state pursues is the manner of education, not its goals. Hence, the state's narrow interest in maintaining the certification requirement must be weighed against the DeJonges' fundamental right of free exercise of religion.[48]

In a further application of the "compelling interest test," the Court found that,

> The State, therefore, must establish that enforcing the certification requirement, without exception, is *essential* to insure the education required by the compulsory education law. *U.S. v. Lee*, 455 U.S. 252, 257-258... If less intrusive means fulfill the government's purported interest, then an exemption must be granted and the alternative implemented.[49]

The State had failed to "provide one scintilla of evidence that the DeJonge children have suffered for the want of certified teachers."[50] The Court properly found the DeJonges were satisfying the state's interest without certified teachers, and therefore teacher certification was not essential.

The Supreme Court relied on studies supplied by HSLDA in order to find that teacher certification is not essential for children to be educated. One study specifically cited in the decision by the Supreme Court is a study by Dr. Brian Ray of the National Home Education Research Institute. Dr. Ray found that there is no positive correlation between the student's performance and the teacher's qualifications. The Court also relied on research supplied in HSLDA's brief which demonstrated that Michigan was the last state still to require teacher certification of home schoolers.[51] This evidence

---

48. *Id.*
49. *Id.*, at 140.
50. *Id.*
51. *Id.*, at 141.

helped them decide that certification was not the least restrictive means of satisfying the State's interest.

The Court also held that the religious home school family does *not* have the burden of proving that alternatives exist. It is the state's burden. The Court explained:

> Furthermore, the court of appeals erroneously placed the burden of proof upon the DeJonges. The court of appeals, by requiring that the individual burdened by governmental regulation prove that alternatives exist, while at the same time accepting at face value unsubstantiated assertions by the state, has turned constitutional jurisprudence on its head. Our citizens need not "propose an alternative" to be afforded their constitutional liberties. *Lee, supra,* 455 U.S. 257-258... *Yoder, supra* 406 U.S. 233-234... We are persuaded that the burden of proof correctly placed in the instant case is fatal to the state's certification requirement.[52]

The Court concluded by stating:

> We believe that the DeJonges are the best judges of which regulations are the most burdensome and least intrusive upon their religion. To entertain the notion that either this Court or the State has the insight to interpret the DeJonges' religion more correctly than they is simply an arrogant pretention.[53]

Summarizing its decision, the court said:

> ...We conclude that the historical underpinnings of the First Amendment to the U.S. Constitution and the case law in support of it compels the conclusion that the imposition of the certification requirement upon the DeJonges violates the Free Exercise Clause. We so conclude because we find that the certification requirement is not essential to nor is it the least restrictive means of achieving the State's

---

52. *Id.,* at 143.
53. *Id.*

claimed interest. Thus, we reaffirm that sphere of inviable conscience and belief which is the mark of a free people. *Weisman,* 505 U.S. at ___. . . We hold that the teacher certification requirement is an unconstitutional violation of the Free Exercise Clause of the First Amendment as applied to families whose religious convictions prohibit the use of certified instructors. Such families, therefore, are exempt from the dictates of the teacher certification requirements.[54]

The ruling in *DeJonge* is a textbook case accurately demonstrating the proper way the "compelling interest test" should be applied when religious beliefs clash with state regulations.

Religious Freedom Restoration Act

This "compelling interest test" was drastically weakened by the United States Supreme Court in the *Employment Division* v. *Smith* case.[55] The court gave the lowest level of protection to religious liberty — one of the foundational freedoms of home schooling. Under this ruling, a state could override an individual's right to freely exercise his religious beliefs merely by proving that its regulation was "reasonable."

However, the Home School Legal Defense Association along with the American Civil Liberties Union and a broad coalition of legal and religious organizations successfully persuaded the United States Congress to enact H.R. 1308, the Religious Freedom Restoration Act (RFRA), on November 16, 1993. The RFRA reiterated a 1963 decision (*Sherbert v. Verner*) in which the Supreme Court held that in order for a state's regulation to prevail over an individual's right to freely exercise his religious belief,

---

54. *Id.,* at 144.
55. *Employment Division* v. *Smith,* 494 U.S. 872 (1990). See Chapter 3 for a more detailed description of *Smith.*

the state had to prove that its regulation was essential to achieve a compelling interest. In addition, the state had to provide evidence that it was using the least restrictive means to accomplish this compelling interest. Under this high standard of review, religious freedom was usually upheld over restrictive state regulations. The RFRA essentially reversed the *Smith* case restoring in full the "compelling interest test" established in *Sherbert* v. *Verner* and the long line of United State Supreme Court cases discussed above.

The RFRA or Public Law 103-141 stated:

SECTION 1. SHORT TITLE.
This Act may be cited as the "Religious Freedom Restoration Act of 1993."

SEC. 2. CONGRESSIONAL FINDINGS AND DECLARATION OF PURPOSES.
(a) Findings.—The Congress finds that—
(1) the framers of the Constitution, recognizing free exercise of religion as an unalienable right, secured its protection in the First Amendment to the Constitution;
(2) laws "neutral" toward religion may burden religious exercise as surely as laws intended to interfere with religious exercise;
(3) governments should not substantially burden religious exercise without compelling justification;
(4) in *Employment Division v. Smith*, 494 U.S. 872 (1990) the Supreme Court virtually eliminated the requirement that the government justify burdens on religious exercise imposed by laws neutral toward religion; and
(5) the compelling interest test as set forth in prior Federal court rulings is a workable test for striking sensible balances between religious liberty and competing prior governmental interests.
(b) Purposes.— The purposes of this Act are—
(1) to restore the compelling interest test as set forth in *Sherbert* v. *Verner*, 374 U.S. 398 (1963) and *Wisconsin v. Yoder*, 406 U.S. 205 (1972) and to guarantee its application in all

cases where free exercise of religion is substantially burdened; and

(2) to provide a claim or defense to persons whose religious exercise is substantially burdened by government.

SEC. 3. FREE EXERCISE OF RELIGION PROTECTED.

(a) In General.— Government shall not substantially burden a person's exercise of religion even if the burden results from a rule of general applicability, except as provided in subsection (b).

(b) Exception.— Government may substantially burden a person's exercise of religion only if it demonstrates that application of the burden to the person—

(1) is in furtherance of a compelling governmental interest; and

(2) is the least restrictive means of furthering that compelling governmental interest.

(c) Judicial Relief.— A person whose religious exercise has been burdened in violation of this section may assert that violation as a claim or defense in a judicial proceeding and obtain appropriate relief against a government.

Standing to assert a claim or defense under this section shall be governed by the general rules of standing under article III of the Constitution.

SEC. 4...[56]

SEC. 5. DEFINITIONS.

... (3) the term "demonstrates" means meets the burdens of going forward with the evidence and of persuasion; and

---

56. SEC. 4. ATTORNEYS FEES.

(a) Judicial Proceedings.— Section 722 of the Revised Statutes (42 U.S.C. 1988) is amended by inserting "the Religious Freedom Restoration Act of 1993," before "or title VI of the Civil Rights Act of 1964".

(b) Administrative Proceedings.— Section 504(b)(1)(C) of title 5, United States Code, is amended—

(1) by striking "and" at the end of clause (ii);

(2) by striking the semicolon at the end of clause (iii) and inserting ", and"; and

(3) by inserting "(iv) the Religious Freedom Restoration Act of 1993;" after clause (iii).

(4) the term "exercise of religion" means the exercise of religion under the First Amendment to the Constitution.[57]

This Act secured protection of religious liberty for all citizens. Parents who home schooled their children for religious reasons clearly benefited from the passage of the RFRA.

Unfortunately, on June 25, 1997, the U.S. Supreme Court, by a 6-3 majority, ruled the Religious Freedom Restoration Act (RFRA) unconstitutional as applied to the states in *City of Boerne v. Flores* (117 S.Ct. 2157, 138 L.Ed. 2d. 624). After the city of Boerne denied a building permit to a church because the church building was located in a historic district, Catholic Archbishop Flores of San Antonio appealed this decision based on his belief that this denial of the church's right to expand to accomodate its growing congregation violated the RFRA.

However, in the *City of Boerne* case, the Supreme Court held that the power of Congress under Section 5 of the 14th Amendment is limited to "enforcing the provisions of the Fourteenth Amendment." In the Court's opinion, Congress does not have the authority to determine what constitutes a constitutional violation. The Court upheld that the RFRA went too far in attempting to change the substantive law of constitutional protections. According to the *Boerne* decision, Congress can make determinations as to the proper interpretation of the Constitution, but courts ultimately have the authority to determine if Congress has exceeded its own constitutional bounds. In other words, the Supreme Court, not Congress, is the final arbiter in interpreting the Constitution.

Justices Rehnquist, Scalia, and Thomas joined with the majority in knocking the first amendment down from its lofty fundamental right status to a simple "garden variety" category. The Court ruled that only when a person's claim to freely exercise a religious belief is combined with another fundamental right still receiving the pro-

---

57. Public Law 103-141, Religious Freedom Act of 1993.

tection of the compelling interest test (in a "hybrid situation") such as freedom of speech, freedom of the press, or the fundamental right of parents to direct the education and upbringing of their children, will it be given more than a simple "reasonable test."

Nonetheless, some states are beginning to fight back by passing state religious freedom acts to counter the *City of Boerne* decision, and restore the compelling interest test to religious freedom claims in state courts. Appendix III provides more details on the events leading to the *City of Boerne* decision and the trend across the states to pass these religious freedom acts.

Conclusion

The Free Exercise Clause, when combined with the parents' fundamental rights to direct the upbringing of their children, is an important defense to families who are home schooling for religious reasons. In addition, the "compelling interest test," when properly applied by the court, can carve out an exemption for the home schooler from the particular, onerous requirement. However, as seen in Chapter 5, many courts, in the past, have tried to circumvent this test by applying the wrong test.

Nonetheless, with the victory for home schools before the Michigan Supreme Court and other courts, home schools need to continue to raise the Free Exercise of Religion defense with the expectation that the courts will properly apply the "compelling interest test" and grant a religious exemption.

When the Free Exercise of Religion defense is combined with the fundamental right of parental liberty guaranteed by the 14th Amendment, home schoolers are protected by this "hybrid" right which requires the application of the compelling interest test.

5 Religious Freedom Case Decisions Against Home Education

In the previous chapters, it was mentioned that there have been several major state court cases which have been decided against parents' rights in the area of home schooling and private schooling. It is important to review some of these cases in order to have a balanced view of how the courts have ruled in the area of home schooling. However, nearly every one of these negative cases has a major constitutional flaw. Some of these cases have wrongly upheld teacher certification requirements, approval requirements, and various other controls against home schools and private schools.

The problem with many of these cases is that they misapply the "compelling interest test" in direct contradiction to United States Supreme Court precedence. These cases against home schooling either apply the wrong constitutional test (a reasonableness test) or ignore the evidentiary requirements of the "least restrictive" burden of the state.

Home schoolers are not alone in their attempts to be free from excessive state regulations; rather they are in very good company since, they follow the precedents set by the United States Supreme Court instead of the erroneous holdings reached by various state courts. Below are several examples of these state cases.

U.S. Supreme Court Condemnation of the Reasonableness Test

The largest group of cases against home schools makes the error of applying a "reasonable or rational relationship test" to the fundamental right of parents to control their children's education and exercise their religious beliefs. For example, using the "reasonableness test," if a home schooler opposed teacher certification based on his religious beliefs and was taken to court, the prosecution would only have to prove that teacher certification was "reasonable" and "rationally-related" to the state's interest that children be educated. Of course, a teacher certification requirement is "reasonable" since all the public schools use certified teachers. The prosecutor, therefore, could easily prove that teacher certification is "reasonable," and the home schooler, with his fundamental, constitutional right to home school would lose his case and have to stop home schooling.

The United States Supreme Court understood the danger of such an easy means for the state to trample fundamental rights in education, so it has repeatedly condemned the application of the "reasonableness test" to fundamental rights:

> And when the interests of parenthood are combined with a Free Exercise claim...more than merely *a reasonable relationship* to some purpose within the competency of the State is required to sustain the validity of the State's requirement under the First Amendment.[1]

In *West Virginia State Board of Education* v. *Barnette*,[2] the U.S. Supreme Court expressly stated that *all* fundamental rights, including the free exercise of religion cannot be infringed by a mere show-

---

1. *Yoder, supra*, 406 U.S., at 233. Also see *Sherbert, supra*, 374 U.S., at 406 and *Hobbie, supra*, 94 L.Ed.2d, at 198.
2. *Barnette*, 319 U.S. 624, 639 (1942).

ing of a "rational basis" for an enactment. When the "compelling interest" test was first completely articulated in *Sherbert v. Verner*, the Court held:

> It is basic that no showing merely of a rational relationship to some colorable state interest would suffice [to infringe a First Amendment right].[3]

The actual test which should be applied is the "compelling interest test which requires the state to prove with evidence that (1) its regulation is "essential" or "necessary" to fulfill the state's interest in education that children become literate and self-sufficient, and (2) its regulation is the "least restrictive means" to fulfilling its interest in education. For instance, a law requiring home school parents to take a teacher's exam (like North Dakota's) would not be the least restrictive, since 49 other states do not require such a high qualifications standard. This two-part burden on the state provides the protection home schoolers need to freely operate, making it very difficult for the state to take away or severely regulate parents' right to teach their own children. However, courts have, in the past, circumvented this test as seen below.

Court Decisions Which Erroneously Apply the Reasonableness Test

In the *Sheridan Road Baptist Church* case, the Court of Appeals of Michigan upheld a teacher certification requirement over the religious objection of church schools on the grounds that:

> the issue is not whether there is a compelling state interest in any individual regulation *but* whether the individual regulations [requiring teacher certification] are

---

3. *Sherbert*, 374 U.S., at 406.

reasonable means to give effect to a broader compelling state interest-in this case the providing of an education to all children. For the reasons stated herein, we believe the regulations are a *reasonable* exercise of state authority in the field of education.[4]

In other words, the Court of Appeals held that the state need only show that the certification requirement is theoretically "reasonably related" to the furtherance of the state's interest in "educated citizens" to justify the infringement of parents' and the church's First Amendment rights. (This application of the "reasonable relations" test, however, was later vigorously condemned by three dissenting Michigan Supreme Court justices in a split decision (3-3) in *Sheridan Road* v. *Department of Education* in 1986.[5]) On May 25, 1993, this precedent by the Michigan Court of Appeals in *Sheridan Road* was over turned by a majority of the Michigan Supreme Court in *People* v. *DeJonge*.[6] (See Chapter 4 for a full analysis of this case.) The Michigan Supreme Court in *DeJonge* restored the proper application of the "compelling interest test," rather than the "reasonableness test," to the religious freedom claims of a home school family that objected to the state's teacher certification requirement for all teachers.

Similar to the earlier erroneous precedent by the Michigan Court of Appeals is the Supreme Court of Nebraska's decision in *Nebraska* v. *Faith Baptist Church.* In this case, the court enforced a teacher certification requirement against a Christian school and parents who had proved that certification burdened their religious beliefs. The court stated:

> ... we think it cannot fairly be disputed that such a requirement [teacher certification] is neither arbitrary *nor unrea-*

---

4. *Sheridan Road Baptist Church* v. *Dept. of Education*, 348 N.W. at 274 (1984).

5. 396 N.W.2d 373, 422-423 (Mich. 1986).

6. *DeJonge*, 501 N.W. 2d 127 (Mich. 1993).

sonable; ... We believe it goes without saying that the State has a compelling interest in the quality and ability of those who are to teach its young people. [emphasis added].[7]

In *Johnson* v. *Charles City*, the Supreme Court of Iowa made an *identical* ruling to *Faith Baptist* and upheld teacher certification requirements against the convictions of church schools by merely concluding "we agree with the views expressed in *State ex rel. Douglas* v. *Faith Baptist Church*, et al. ... 1981.[8] Then the court proceeded to quote the paragraph above from *Faith Baptist* as the sole grounds for denying the religious school's Free Exercise rights and Fourteenth Amendment rights. No analysis of whether the burdensome requirements were essential or least restrictive was ever performed.

This reliance on the Nebraska Supreme Court's *Faith Baptist* decision "snowballs" even further with the U.S. District Court in Iowa in *Fellowship Baptist Church* v. *Benton*. In this case, the court upheld certification requirements that burdened several church schools' religious beliefs, by relying on *Johnson*, which relied on *Faith Baptist*, which erroneously applied the reasonable relationship test instead of the mandated compelling interest/least restrictive test. [9] The court in *Fellowship*, like the Iowa Supreme Court, did not independently apply the proper "compelling interest test" to the facts of that case.

In North Dakota, the same "snowball" effect occurred. The first case, *North Dakota* v. *Shaver*, dealing with a church school's First Amendment objection to the state's restrictive teacher certification requirements, ruled in favor of the state based on the erroneous application of the "reasonable relationship" test. In ruling against the Free Exercise objections to teacher certification, the North Dakota Supreme Court stated:

---

7. *Faith Baptist*, 301 N.W.2d 571, 779 (Neb, 1981).
8. *Charles City*, 368 N.W. 2d 74, 81 (1985).
9. *Fellowship Baptist*, 620 F.Supp. 308 (1985).

> For this reason, we believe that the right of parents to direct the upbringing and education of their children is subject to reasonable state regulation pursuant to the state's police powers. We have not been shown wherein the state's laws are *unreasonable*.... the parents have not shown how the legitimate and compelling interest of the state in educating its people has been *unreasonably* pursued. [emphasis added].[10]

In *North Dakota* v. *Rivinius*,[11] and *North Dakota* v. *Patzer*,[12] the North Dakota Supreme Court upheld certification requirements against established religious beliefs of parents who chose to home school because the government regulations were not "unreasonable" in furthering the state's interest in education. In *Rivinius*, the court concluded that the state's certification laws did not "unreasonably interfere" with the parents religious beliefs, and in *Patzer*, the court concluded:

> We believe that teacher certification requirement for instructors in public, nonpublic, or home schools is a *reasonably* narrow one and amply justified.[13]

Based on the "reasonableness" of the requirement, the court found teacher certification "to be among the least personally intrusive methods now available to satisfy the state's prime interest." (This finding is nonsensical after reviewing the research in Chapter 10 which demonstrates no positive correlation between teacher qualifications and student performance.)[14] In both cases, the North Dakota Supreme Court relied on its earlier erroneous application of the reasonable relationship test established in *Shaver*.

Another "snowball" effect began with *Maine* v. *McDonough*. In the *McDonough* case, the Maine Supreme Court was dealing

---

10. *North Dakota* v. *Shaver*, 294 N.W.2d 883, 899 (1980).
11. *Rivinius*, 328 N.W.2d 220, 231 (1982).
12. *Patzer*, 382 N.W.2d 631 (N.D. 1986).
13. *Id.*, at 639.
14. *Id.*

with a home schooling case where the parents specifically stated that they did not base their claim to teach their children at home on the Free Exercise Clause of the First Amendment.[15] As a result, that court applied a "reasonableness" standard. The court held concerning prior approval, "... we do not find anything unreasonable in that requirement." [16]

Unfortunately, at least two other cases relied on the holding of *McDonough* to rule against parents' Free Exercise claims even though *McDonough* had nothing to do with the First Amendment. Not to mention it even applied the wrong test to the Fourteenth Amendment right of parental liberty . In *Ohio* v. *Schmidt*, the Supreme Court of Ohio cited *McDonough* when it ruled:

> We hold that the requirement... that parents must seek the approval of the local superintendent for their home education program in order to obtain an excuse from the compulsory attendance laws, *reasonably* furthers the state's interest in the education of its citizens and does not infringe upon the free exercise of religion. [emphasis added].[17]

Similarly, in *Care of Protection of Charles* , the Supreme Judicial Court of Massachusetts declined to consider the parents' Free Exercise claims and upheld the "approval process" for home schools citing *McDonough* as support for their reasoning.[18]

As a result, the fact that the prior approval requirement or teacher certification may be "reasonable" to a court or that it may be one of many different ways to fulfill the state's interest in education is *irrelevant*. When confronted with fundamental rights of parents or religious beliefs that are being burdened by the restrictive requirement, the state must *prove* that the requirement is both (1) "essential" to fulfilling the state's interest in education, and (2) that it is

---

15. *McDonough,* 468 A.2d 977, 979 (1983).
16. *Id.,* at 980.
17. *Schmidt,* 505 N.E.2d 627, 629-630 (1987).
18. *Charles,* 504 N.E.2d 592, 600 (1987).

"the least restrictive means" of fulfilling that interest. If the state does not satisfy these two burdens, the home school family should be exempted from the restrictive requirements.

Most of these state cases supporting the erroneous application of the reasonableness test and ruling against home schoolers, have been practically "mooted" by intervention of the legislature in enacting new "less restrictive" laws for home schools and church schools.[19]

State Regulations of Home Schools Must Be Essential and the Least Restrictive Means, Not Merely Reasonable

In conclusion, as previously discussed in Chapter 4, the Supreme Court has held that the regulations must be "essential" and "the least restrictive means" in order to survive constitutional scrutiny. This standard is outlined further in the "Religious Freedom Restoration Act" enacted by Congress in 1993 (See Chapter 4.) Most regulations may be "reasonable," few are "essential" "or the "least restrictive means."

As the United States Supreme Court said in *Widmar* v. *Vincent*[20] "the state must show that its *regulation* is *necessary* to serve a compelling state interest...."and therefore,"...more than merely a reasonable relationship to some purpose within the competency of the state is required to sustain the validity of the requirement under the First Amendment."[21]

In court decisions where the "compelling interest test" is properly applied as seen in Chapter 4, religious home schoolers nearly

---

19. See Revised Stat. of Nebraska §79-1701(3); N.D. Century Code §15-34.1-03; and Iowa H.F. 455(1991).

20. *Widmar,* 454 U.S. 263, 270 (1981).

21. *Yoder,* 406 U.S. at 233.

always win, thereby preventing the state from prohibiting parents from exercising their right to home school.

A parent's right to control and direct the education and religious upbringing of his children is a fundamental right, not a state granted privilege. Throughout the history of the United States, parents have been recognized as having a preferred status in controlling the education of their minor children. The state regulations, if burdensome to parents, must be more than simply reasonable. Strict scrutiny must be applied by the courts, and the state has the burden of proving, with evidence, that its regulation is "essential" and the "least restrictive means" to achieve a "compelling state interest."

6 Restrictions Are Often Found Unconstitutionally Void for Vagueness

When many of the compulsory attendance laws were enacted in the early 1900s, home schooling was ignored. The laws required children between certain ages to attend either public or private school, but no exemption was provided for home schools. When home schoolers in those states tried to operate as private schools, they were prosecuted. However, some of the state courts, as discussed in Chapter 7, properly ruled that since a private school is a "place of learning;" a home school could freely operate as a private school and therefore legally satisfy the law.

In several of the other states that did not have a home school alternative, the courts followed a different course. They ruled that the compulsory attendance statutes were "void for vagueness" and subsequently struck down the laws as unconstitutional. These decisions fall into two categories: (1) either the definition of the term "private school" was determined by the courts to be unconstitutionally vague as in Wisconsin, Georgia, and California; or (2) some other language in the law such as the term "equivalent instruction" or "properly qualified" was found by the courts to be vague, as in Minnesota, Pennsylvania, Missouri, and Iowa.

This brings the reader to the question: "What exactly is a vague law?"

Identification of a Vague Law

A vague compulsory attendance law is one where the local school district or school official is given virtually unlimited **discretion** to define key terms in the law, or generally has the freedom to "legislate" his own home school policy. For instance, in Pennsylvania before the *Jeffery* decision, 501 different superintendents were given authority, by the law, to determine if home school instruction was "satisfactory." Nearly each of the 501 school districts had different restrictions on home schoolers, covering virtually every kind of requirement imaginable. Depending on the particular superintendent in power at a given time in the school district a family lived in, home schools were either prosecuted or left alone. Many home schoolers had to flee one school district where home schooling was never "satisfactory" to another school district where home schooling was at least tolerated. In Pennsylvania in 1988, the Home School Legal Defense Association alone was representing nearly thirty home school families in court and hundreds of others who were threatened with prosecution.

Other states, like Missouri prior to the *Ellis* decision, required instruction to be "equivalent." Similarly, each superintendent arbitrarily created, according to his own whim, a definition of "equivalent." In many school districts, the superintendent made it impossible for a home schooler to be able to satisfy his arbitrary definition of equivalent instruction.

The United States Supreme Court has dealt with this issue on numerous occasions and has set clear guidelines for determining whether a statute is unconstitutionally vague under the Due Process Clause of the Constitution.[1]

---

1. When parents are home schooling for religious reasons under the First Amendment, "special scrutiny" must be applied whenever a vague compulsory attendance statute imposes criminal penalties which tend to operate to inhibit the exercise of those freedoms. See *Kolender* v. *Lawson*, 461 U.S. 352, 358 n. 8 (1983).

1. A law is vague if persons of average intelligence, such as home school parents, are not put on notice as to what is required or what is forbidden. Furthermore, "persons of common intelligence must not be left to guess at the meaning of a statute nor differ as to its application."[2] For example, in Pennsylvania prior to 1989, home schoolers were required by law to be "properly qualified" but neither the home schoolers nor the superintendents knew what that meant. Many home school families stayed "underground," (did not notify the school district), because they did not know if the superintendent would interpret "properly qualified" to mean certified, holding a college degree, high school diploma, or something else.

2. A law is vague if arbitrary and discriminatory enforcement is permitted. In other words, if a superintendent, under the law, is free to discriminate against home schoolers and create his own arbitrary standards for home schoolers, the law is too vague, lacking the necessary explicit standards. Furthermore, courts have consistently held that a law is vague if the officials charged with enforcement and application of the law are permitted to resolve questions "on an ad hoc and subjective basis." In short, the fundamental right of parents to home school cannot be denied by the enforcement of a vague law that authorizes such a denial purely on the whim of a superintendent or other school official.

The Landmark U.S. Supreme Court Which Defined Vagueness

In a landmark case, the U.S. Supreme Court summarized its doctrine on vagueness in *Grayned* v. *City of Rockford*.[3] In that case the Court said:

---

2. *Connally* v. *General Construction Co.* 269 U.S. 385, 391, 46 S.Ct. 126, 127, 70 L.Ed. 322 (1925).
3. *Grayned,* 408 U.S. 104 (1972).

It is a basic principle of due process that an enactment is void for vagueness if its prohibitions are not clearly defined. Vague laws offend several important values. First, because we assume that man is free to steer between lawful and unlawful conduct, we insist that laws give the person of ordinary intelligence a reasonable opportunity to know what is prohibited, so that he may act accordingly. Vague laws may trap the innocent by not providing fair warning. Second, if arbitrary and discriminatory enforcement is to be prevented, laws must provide explicit standards for those who apply them. A vague law impermissibly delegates basic policy matters to policemen, judges and juries for resolution on an ad hoc basis, with the attendant dangers of arbitrary and discriminatory application. Third, but related, where a statute "abut[s] upon sensitive First Amendment freedoms," it "operates to inhibit the exercise of those freedoms." Uncertain meanings inevitably lead citizens to " 'steer far wider of the unlawful zone' ... than if the boundaries of the forbidden areas were clearly marked."[4]

Unfettered Discretion Is Unconstitutional

Of the two major identifying characteristics of a vague law listed above, unfettered discretion in the hands of superintendents to define the law and create arbitrary requirements for home schools, is the most dangerous characteristic to the home schooler.

The Supreme Court in *Interstate Circuit* v. *Dallas*,[5] condemned such discretion:

> [L]egislation must not be so vague, the language so loose as to leave those who have to apply it too wide a discretion. ... *Kingsley Int'l Pictures Corp.* v. *Regents*, 360 U.S., at 694.

---

4. *Id.*, 408 U.S., at 108-109.
5. *Interstate Circuit,* 390 U.S. 676, 684 (1968).

Oftentimes, the problem with state compulsory attendance laws is that the "language [is] so loose as to leave those who have to apply it too wide a discretion," *Id.*, which results in the arbitrary denial of parental rights in education. Many of these types of vague laws yield discriminatory results: (1) dozens of differing definitions of teacher qualifications, (2) various monitoring procedures such as home visits by school officials, (3) all types, times, and places of student testing, (4) variety of progress reports, and (5) arbitrary periodic meetings.

In many instances, these statutes allow the opinion of the superintendent to control a decision as to whether parents will be allowed to exercise the fundamental constitutional rights of directing the upbringing of their children and the free exercise of their religion as guaranteed by the First and Fourteenth Amendments of the U.S. Constitution. (See Chapters 3 and 4 for a full discussion of these constitutional rights.)

The principles of due process of law are violated by such a system. It should never depend on the opinion of a government official as to whether or not a person in this country is permitted to exercise a constitutional right.

For example, in the case of *Hague v. CIO*.[6] the local Director of Public Safety had the unfettered discretion to decide who would be allowed to use the city's public parks for rallies, preaching, and all other free speech purposes. The ordinance granting him such discretion allowed him to deny permission if "on his mere opinion that such refusal will prevent riots, disturbances or disorderly assemblage."[7] The United States Supreme Court struck down this statutory scheme, not because it wanted to protect riots or disturbances; rather, the Court held that this statute permitted "uncontrolled official suppression" of the constitutional rights of others based upon the mere opinion of a government official.

---

6. *Hague,* 307 U.S. 496 (1939).
7. *Id.,* at 516.

Applying this to home schooling, the mere opinion of a local superintendent cannot be permitted to control the exercise of this right any more than an official can control the right of free speech in a public park.[8]

In conclusion, one of the most common characteristics of a vague statute is, in the words of the United States Supreme Court, one which "impermissibly delegates basic policy matters to policemen, judges and juries for resolution on an ad hoc basis, with the attendant dangers of arbitrary and discriminatory application." [9]

In home schooling matters, superintendents rather than policemen are involved, but the constitutional principles are the same. In states with vague compulsory attendance laws, a family is in compliance with the compulsory attendance law only if what they are doing is satisfactory to the local superintendent. If they are doing something which the local superintendent deems unsatisfactory, then they are in violation of the law. Violation of these compulsory attendance statutes is a criminal offense. As a result, in these states with vague laws, a home schooler is guilty of a crime for the sole reason that he has failed to satisfy a particular public school official who may create whatever standards he chooses. In fact, many school superintendents in these states have no written standards. Even those superintendents who do have some written standards have written them vaguely, allowing them to apply the standards differently to different home schoolers. Therefore, home schoolers could be and are criminally charged for violating standards which exist only in the mind of a local superintendent.

---

8. Furthermore, we think it important to note that the High Court has held that there is no exception to the rule prohibiting vague statutes even if the goal is protecting children. The Supreme Court, in *Interstate Circuit, supra*, said:

> Nor is it an answer to an argument that a particular regulation of expression is vague to say that it was adopted for the salutary purpose of protecting children.

390 U.S., at 689.

9. *Grayned, supra*, 408 U.S., at 108-109.

Home School Court Decisions Declaring Statutes Unconstitutionally Vague

Six states have recently been confronted with successful constitutional challenges to compulsory attendance statutes by families who were teaching their own children at home.

Minnesota

The Supreme Court of Minnesota in 1985 in *State* v. *Newstrom*,[10] made a ruling in a home schooling case that Minnesota's compulsory attendance law was unconstitutionally vague. The statute provided that students must be:

...taught by teachers whose qualifications are essentially equivalent to the minimum standards for public school teachers of the same grades or subjects....

The Minnesota Supreme Court struck down this statute on grounds of constitutional vagueness of the term "essentially equivalent." The Court said that the term "essentially equivalent" was too vague to "serve as a basis for criminal conviction" and thus violated the right of due process as guaranteed under the Fourteenth Amendment.[11]

Wisconsin

In the case of *State of Wisconsin* v. *Popanz*,[12] the Supreme Court of Wisconsin held that the former compulsory attendance law was "void for vagueness insofar as it fails to define private school."[13] That statute required attendance at a public or private school without any definition of what constituted a private school for the pur-

---

10. *Newstrom*, 371 N.W.2d 533 (Minn. 1985).
11. *Newstrom*, 371 N.W.2d at 533.
12. *Popanz*, 112 Wis.2d 166, 332 N.W.2d 750 (1983).
13. *Popanz*, 332 N.W.2d at 756.

poses of the statute. Superintendents who were prosecuting home schoolers improperly argued that home schools could not be private schools. But the Court said:

> The persons who must obey the law should not have to guess at what the phrase "private school" means. They should have some objective standards to guide them in their attempts to "steer between lawful and unlawful conduct." *Grayned v. City of Rockford*, 408 U.S. 104, 108, 92 S.Ct. 2294, 2298, 33 L.Ed.2d 222 (1972). Furthermore, standards cannot lie only in the minds of persons whose duty it is to enforce the laws. We must conclude that the statute fails to provide fair notice to those who would seek to obey it and also lacks sufficient standards for proper enforcement.[14]

Georgia

Similarly, the Supreme Court of Georgia in *Roemhild v. State*,[15] ruled its compulsory attendance law unconstitutionally void for vagueness. Since the law did not provide for home schools, many home schoolers tried to operate as private schools, but the state continued to prosecute them. The Supreme Court of Georgia finally declared in *Roemhild*:

> We conclude that the statute is not sufficiently definite to provide a person of ordinary intelligence, who desires to avoid its penalties, fair notice of what constitutes a private school...

The Court went on to note:

> Furthermore, the statute violates a second due process value in that it impermissibly delegates to local law enforcement officials, judges, and juries the policy decision of what constitutes a "private school."[16]

---

14. *Id.,* at 756.
15. *Roemhild,* 251 Ga. 569, 308 S.E.2d 154 (1983).
16. *Id.,* 308 S.E.2d at 158.

Missouri

The federal district court for the Eastern District of Missouri ruled in 1985 in *Ellis v. O'Hara*[17] that the Missouri compulsory attendance statute was unconstitutionally vague in a case brought by home schooling families. In that case, the compulsory attendance statute authorized home education which was "substantially equivalent to the instruction given children of like age in the day schools in the locality in which the child resides."[18] The federal court held:

Under the Missouri scheme of legislation, cases of suspected educational neglect in the home school context are turned over to the appropriate local school district for investigation. Following the investigation, the school district has discretion to transfer responsibility of the case to the prosecutor. § 210.167 R.S. Mo. (1984). The local school district is thus initially charged with ensuring that parents comply with the requirements of § 167.031, and that children educated at home receive a substantially equivalent education to the day schools in the particular locality. Nowhere is substantially equivalent defined, however, or are regulations promulgated which clarify its meaning. Nor have the Missouri courts furnished edification regarding the meaning of the statute. In this respect, the statute subjects the exercise of a fundamental right to an unascertainable standard. *Coates v. City of Cincinnati*, 402 U.S. 611, 614 (1971). The parents have not been equipped with

---

17. 612 F.Supp 379 (E.D. Mo. 1985). *Ellis*, was "reversed" by an order of the Eighth Circuit. 802 F.2d 462 (8th Cir. 1986). The published decision gives only the word "reversed" as a docket entry. From reviewing the actual opinion of the Eighth Circuit, it is obvious that the decision was reversed to permit the district court to make an inquiry into the issue of mootness in light of a newly enacted Missouri statute which eliminated the vagueness of the compulsory attendance statute. The Eighth Circuit, in another case, affirmed a ruling virtually similar to the ruling on the vagueness issue in *Ellis*. See, *Fellowship Baptist Church v. Benton*, 620 F.Supp. 308 (S.D. Iowa 1985); 815 F.2d 486 (8th Cir. 1986).
18. § 167.031 R.S.Mo. (1978).

an adequate definition of substantially equivalent to inform them of their obligations under the statute. Of even greater significance, however, is that the Legislature has not provided minimal guidelines for law enforcement. *Kolender v. Lawson*, 461 U.S. at 358. This statute represents a prime example of legislation which yields an unacceptable amount of discretion to officials charged with its enforcement. The statute, therefore, does not comply with due process requirements, and is unconstitutionally vague.

In other words, state compulsory attendance laws which "subject the exercise of a fundamental right to an unascertainable standard" as well as "yield[ing] an unacceptable amount of discretion to officials charged with" the enforcement of the law are unconstitutional.

Furthermore, in *Ellis* v. *O'Hara* the Court summarized many of the United States Supreme Court cases condemning vague laws:

A statute is unconstitutionally vague when it commands or prescribes conduct in terms so vague that persons "of common intelligence must necessarily guess at its meaning and differ as to its application." *Connally v. General Construction Co.*, 269 U.S. 385, 391 (1926). *See also, Zwickler v. Koata*, 389 U.S. 241 249 (1967). The vagueness doctrine also applies to statutes which lack minimal guidelines for their enforcement. *Kolender v. Lawson*, 461 U.S. 352, 358 (1983); *Smith v. Goguen*, 415 U.S. at 575.... A more stringent vagueness test applies to statutes which affect the exercise of constitutionally protected rights and to statutes which carry criminal penalties. *Village of Hoffman Estates v. The Flipside, Hoffman Estates, Inc.*, 455 U.S. 489, 499 (1982); *Grayned v. City of Rockford*, 408 U.S. at 109.

In applying these principles, this challenge to the Missouri compulsory attendance statute on vagueness grounds commands a stringent scrutiny by this Court because the constitutional right of parents to direct the upbringing of their children and to inculcate religious and educational values in their offspring is implicated. *Wisconsin v. Yoder*, 406 U.S. 205, 232 (1972); *Pierce v. Society of Sisters*, 268 U.S. 510, 53435 (1925).[19]

Iowa

The law of the State of Iowa which previously required "equivalent instruction upon a certified teacher elsewhere,"[20] has been found unconstitutionally void for vagueness for several reasons. In *Iowa v. Trucke*,[21] Supreme Court of Iowa summarized the history of the vagueness to the Iowa law challenges saying:

> In *Johnson v. Charles City Community School Boards*, 368 N.W.2d 74, 80 (Iowa 1985), *cert. denied*, __ U.S. __ (1985) we alluded to such a challenge, observing that "[w]hen the state fails to adequately set necessary minimum standards for private religious schools, the patrons are presented with a ready defense to truancy charges." The United States Court of Appeals for the Eighth Circuit recently confirmed our view, holding the undefined "equivalent instruction" requirement unconstitutionally vague. *Fellowship Baptist Church v. Benton*, 815 F.2d 486, 495-96 (8th Cir. 1987).[22]

The district court in *Fellowship Baptist Church v. Benton*,[23] more thoroughly discussed the reasons that Iowa law was vague. The court said:

> Moreover, the Court finds, in light of the varying interpretations offered by the State and County officials charged with assessing compliance with the law, that the term "equivalent instruction" fails to give notice to the ordinary man

---

19. *Ellis*, 612 F.Supp., at 380-381.
20. Iowa Code § 299.1.
21. *Trucke*, 410 N.W.2d 242 (Iowa 1987).
22. *Id.*
23. *Fellowship Baptist Church*, 620 F.Supp. 308 (S.D. Iowa 1985); aff'd 815 F.2d 486 (8th Cir. 1986).

of what is prohibited by the statute. *See Colten v. Kentucky,* 407 U.S. 104, 110, 92 S.Ct. 1953, 1957, 32 L.Ed.2d 584 (1972).

...

There may be problems when the responsibility of determining equivalent education is placed on local school boards even when it is more closely defined for two reasons.... **[E]ach local school board may still have a different interpretation.**[24]

This is a strong recognition that when interpretation of the law is left up to local school districts, variance, and thus unconstitutional vagueness, is the result. Every district gets to decide for itself what the standards will be.

Pennsylvania

In Pennsylvania, as mentioned above, home schoolers were faced with constant harassment by their local school districts. The law gave the superintendent the power to define if a home school parent was "properly qualified" and whether or not his curriculum was "satisfactory." Since there were 501 school districts, each with its own definitions of these terms, the application of this vague law often led to absurd results.

One of the most ridiculous examples involved a client of the Home School Legal Defense Association (HSLDA), the Smeltzer family, whose child was designated as having various learning disabilities and in need of special education. For some reason, the superintendent allowed the family to home school for three years. At the end of the third year, the child did so well on her standardized achievement tests, that the superintendent labeled her "gifted and talented." However, he and his specialists also determined that the family could no longer handle her education because she was

---

24. *Id.,* at 318. The Iowa Legislature finally resolved the vagueness of the statute by passing regulations that define "equivalent instruction."

now gifted. He therefore disapproved their home school and demanded the child be sent to the public schools. When the family refused, he filed criminal truancy charges against the family.

When HSLDA was informed, it immediately prepared a civil rights complaint asserting the family's constitutional rights, explaining that the superintendent was personally liable for violating their civil rights. A copy of the complaint was sent to the school board's lawyer. By the next day, the Smeltzer's home school program was approved and the charges dropped, before it was necessary to file the civil rights complaint with the court.[25]

Since more and more "brush fires" started across the state with home schoolers being dragged into court, HSLDA filed a civil rights case, *Jeffery* v. *O'Donnell*[26] suing school districts throughout the state. The federal court ruled:

> ... Disparity abounds. What can be satisfactory in one school district could be totally unsatisfactory in another. The ultimate conclusion one must reach concerning tutorial education in Pennsylvania is that, ... the law providing for such an education is unconstitutionally vague. ... A person of ordinary intelligence cannot reasonably steer between the lawful and the unlawful to avoid criminal prosecution. There exists no standard for determining who is a qualified tutor or what is a satisfactory curriculum in any district. Superintendents of school districts, while exercising a legitimate and constitutional function of managing their districts according to the unique character of each district, nevertheless make their decisions on an *ad hoc* basis which can result in the dangers of arbitrary and discriminatory application. ... The threat to sensitive First Amendment freedoms mandates judicial intrusion in the form of declaring

---

25. *Home School Court Report*, "Pennsylvania Under Fire," Jan.-Feb. 1987 edition, Vol. 3, No. 1, Paeonian Springs, VA. This article also documents many other cases pending in Pennsylvania during that time.

26. Two separate and favorable decisions resulted: *Jeffery*, 702 F.Supp. 513 (M.D. PA 1988) and *Jeffery*, 702 F.Supp. 516 (M.D. PA 1988).

the particular provision of the law unconstitutional for vagueness.[27]

The court declared the law to be unconstitutionally vague as applied to home schoolers, and the final result was that the legislature was forced to rewrite the law to specifically protect home schooling and eliminate the school districts' discretionary powers in approving or disapproving home schools.

In fact, the cases in Missouri, Minnesota, Georgia, and Wisconsin, described above, all resulted in favorable laws which have tremendously reduced the conflict between home schoolers and the state. Only Iowa avoided protecting home schoolers by passing new State Department of Education regulations which made the vague law clear but still overly restrictive. However, in 1991, this law was amended by the Iowa Legislature, removing the requirement for a certified teacher. In fact, Iowa no longer has any teacher qualification requirements for home schoolers under the new law.

Conclusion

Vagueness has continues to be one of the most successful defenses of home schoolers who live in states without specific home school laws. In fact, in Michigan, previously one of the most difficult states in which to home school, a home school mother had been arrested, finger printed, photographed, and charged with criminal truancy. HSLDA filed a "motion to dismiss" in this case called *People* v. *Pebler*. After oral arguments, the court ruled in favor of the home schooler, dismissed the case, and found the Michigan compulsory attendance law "vague and unclear as to what specifically constitutes a violation of that act subjecting a person to criminal prose-

---

27. *Jeffery*, 702 F.Supp. 516, 521.

cution, and Laurel Pebler is entitled to fair notice of what conduct is proscribed by the statute."[28]

Legislation which gives any amount of arbitrary discretion over home schoolers to the public school system should be opposed to avoid this kind of discriminatory treatment. States that have vague laws at present should be carefully monitored and possibly challenged if the law is being used to harass home schoolers.

28. *People* v. *Pebler*, No. 91-0848-SM, St. Joseph County 3-B District Court, Judge William McManus, Order of Dismissal, July 2, 1991.

7 The Right to Home School Protected Under Private School Laws

Before home schools statutes began to be passed in the 1980s, most compulsory attendance laws required children to attend either public school or private school. In some states, the only other alternative was for a child to be instructed by a state certified teacher. No specific statutory option existed for home schools. (In at least twelve states this is still the case, and those states are briefly discussed in Chapter 12.)

As a result, home school families, who were home schooling based on their religious convictions as guaranteed by the First Amendment or their parental rights as guaranteed by the Fourteenth Amendment, were forced to qualify as a private school or, in some instances, become certified to teach as a "private tutor." Qualifying as a public school, of course, was impossible. The rationale was simple. The right of parents to teach their children at home is a constitutional right guaranteed by the First and Fourteenth Amendment. Therefore, to outlaw home schooling altogether would be a violation of a family's constitutional rights. Since teacher certification (under the tutor option) was an overly restrictive requirement which basically prohibited families from home schooling, operating as a private school was the only option that remained.

Home schools needed to be able to operate as private schools in order for the state to fulfill its duty to adequately protect the parents' constitutional right to teach their own children. The purpose of the compulsory attendance laws is to have children educated, and that is what home schooling, operating under the private school status, is accomplishing.

Consequently, many of these type of cases appeared throughout the country as home school families defended their right to exist as a private school, or, in some instances, for their right to exist as a "satellite" of an existing private school. Much precedent was set and most of that precedent favors home schools.

The Meaning of the Word "School"

As can be imagined, the major contention between the home schools and the state was, and continues to be in some states, "what is the actual definition of a private school." Since nearly every state did not define the term "private school" in its statute, some courts, such as the District Court of Appeals in the *Buckner* case in Florida and Arkansas Supreme Court in the *Burrow* case, decided to exceed their bounds and do some legislating.[1] These courts argued that the "ordinary meaning" of the word "school" means an "institution" with a building and children from more than one family. However, both of these decisions were rendered moot (or of no effect) by their respective legislatures which passed, in 1985, specific laws legally protecting home schools.[2]

Contrary to the above courts' claims, the ordinary meaning of the word "school" is a "place of learning." This popular definition

---

1. For instance, in Florida and Arkansas, two state court decisions ruled that the definition of school did not include a home school. *Burrow* v. *State*, 282 Ark. 479, 669 S.W.2d 441 (1984) and *State of Florida* v. *Buckner*, 472 So. 2d 1228, (Fla. Dist. Ct. App. 1985). In both of these decisions, the courts created definitions of private school out of thin air. Since the Arkansas and Florida statutes did not define the term "private school," these courts decided to "legislate" and create a definition that would exclude home schooling. The home school families were convicted even though their home schools satisfied all the statutory requirements for private schools.

2. See Florida Statutes Annotated sections 228.041(34) and 232.02(4) and Arkansas Statutes Annotated section 80-1503.

of "school" is found in many dictionaries and recognized by many other courts around the country. In Black's Law Dictionary, for instance, "school" is defined as "an institution *or* place of instruction or education." Funk and Wagnalls Dictionary defines "school" as "the place in which formal instruction is given." Home schooling definitely fits these descriptions because it is a "place of instruction." Many court cases involving home schoolers being charged with truancy found the home schoolers "not guilty," because their home school met all the requirements for a private school.

Cases Which Recognize Home Schools as Private Schools

In Illinois, for example, the Illinois Supreme Court found that a school in the home was a legitimate private school. *People* v. *Levisen*,[3] The Court declared that a school is:

> a place where instruction is imparted to the young... *the number of persons* being taught does not determine whether a place is a school.[4]

The Court explained further:

> Compulsory education laws are enacted to enforce the natural obligations of parents to provide an education for their young, an obligation which corresponds to the parents' right of control over the child... The object is that all shall be educated not that they shall be educated in any particular manner or place.[5]

Since that decision, thousands of home schools (many with only one or two children) operate freely as private schools in Illinois.

---

3. *Levisen*, 90 N.E.2d 213 (1950).
4. *Levisen*, at 215.
5. *Id.*

In Indiana, the Indiana Appellate Court reached the same conclusions in *State* v. *Peterman*.[6] The Court ruled that a home school has the same status as a private school, leaving home schools virtually unregulated. The Court defined a "school" as:

> a place where instruction is imparted to the young... We do not think that the *number of persons*, whether one or many, makes a place where instruction is imparted any less or any more a school.[7]

In Massachusetts, the Supreme Judicial Court held in favor of a school operating in the home and stated that the object of the compulsory attendance law is "that all children shall be educated, not that they shall be educated in any particular way."[8]

Home schools in many states do fulfill the *object* of the compulsory attendance law *and* meet *all* of the technical requirements of the law for private or church schools.

In California, thousands of home schools operate as private schools. Each year, certain counties take families to court, challenging their right to exist as private schools and stating that their only option is to become certified tutors. However, the courts have sided with the home schoolers. For example, the Home School Legal Defense Association handled the *People* v. *Darrah* and the *People* v. *Black* cases[9] where two home school families were denied the right to operate as private schools, even though they met all the requirements of a private school in California. The Court ruled in favor of the families, finding that the law was unconstitutionally vague and that the families could not be prosecuted for operating as private schools. Nothing in the law prohibited them from being a private school.

---

6. *Peterman*, 70 NE 550 (1904).

7. *Id.,* at 551.

8. *Care and Protection of Charles*, 504 N.E.2d 592, 600 (1987).

9. *Darrah*, No. 853104 and *Black*, No. 853105, Santa Maria Mun. Ct., March 10, 1986.

In Colorado, home schools have a choice to operate under the home school law (Colorado Revised Statutes section 22-33-104.5) or under a private school. The Colorado Court of Appeals in *People in Interest of D.B.*,[10] held that children enrolled in private schools (independent schools) could be taught at home. Once children are enrolled in a private school they are exempt from the compulsory attendance law. "The matter of the sufficiency of the children's attendance is between them [the home schoolers] and the independent school in which they are enrolled."[11]

The Colorado Court of Appeals turned on the word "attend." Since the children are not required to "attend" but only be "enrolled" in the private school, they are free to attend elsewhere (at home) as long as the private school renders the arrangement sufficient.

Home schoolers therefore can choose to operate under a private school as a legal alternative to the home school law.

In Kansas, the Kansas Supreme Court in *State v. Lowry*,[12] found that the particular school in the Lowry home was **not** a proper private school, but only because the school did not meet the minimal state requirements of a private school. The Court stated:

> In order to be classed as a private school, any school in this state must at least meet the course of instruction requirements of KSA 72-1103, and the students must be taught by a competent instructor.[13]

The Court recognized that a private school can exist in the home *if* it meets certain basic requirements.

In 1983, the Kansas Supreme Court again ruled on a case involving a private school operating in a home.[14] In *Sawyer*, the Court held that a system of education which consisted of an unplanned,

---

10. *D.B.*, 767 P. 2d (Colo. App. 1988) at 801.
11. *Id.*, at 802.
12. *Lowry*, 383 P. 2d. 962, (1963),
13. 383 P.2d.962 at 964.
14. *In Interest of Sawyer*, 672 P.2d. 1093.

unscheduled instruction program by a teacher who was not competent did not satisfy the compulsory attendance laws and thus was not a proper private school. The fact that the Sawyers' school was located in the Sawyers' home had no bearing on the Court's reasoning.

Meanwhile, thousands of home schoolers routinely operate as "non-accredited private schools" in Kansas. The trial courts have repeatedly upheld the right of home schools to operate as private schools in spite of the ruling in *Lowry* and *Sawyer*.[15] The lower courts easily distinguish *Lowry* and *Sawyer*, since those cases involved home schools that did *not* meet the requirements of a non-accredited private school. One court, in the *Ahlman* case, found that a family teaching their child at home was legal since they had registered as "nonaccredited private school" and had regular instruction. The court stated:

> the [compulsory attendance] statute does not authorize independent evaluation of the competency of a prima facie private school by local public school officials or local law enforcement authorities, absent clear evidence of a sham or subterfuge involving educational neglect. Children found to be participating in a prima facie private school are not truant under section 72-1111 notwithstanding the fact that such school operates in a private residence.[16]

Furthermore, truancy charges were dismissed against home school parents in Hillsboro, Kansas in the *Jost* case.[17] The Jost family had properly registered their private school and were teaching

---

15. Some of the cases which have found home schools to be legitimate private schools are *In re Jost*, No. 84-C-88 (Marion County District Court 1985); *In re Hardon*, No. 85-JC-9 (Rawlins County Dist. Ct. January 17, 1986); *In re Hastings*, No. 83-JC-1365 (Harvey County District Court 1984); *In re Willms*, No. 87-JC-350 (Shawnee County Dist. Ct., Feb. 12, 1988).

16. *In re Ahlman*, No. 83-JC-1366 (Harvey County Dist. Ct. April 11, 1984, Slip. op.

17. See *In re Jost*, No. 84-C-88, Marion County Dist. Ct. 1985.

their three children in a classroom in their home. The Josts' school met all the statutory requirements of a nonaccredited private school. HSLDA, which handled the case, argued that the Josts' school was a bona fide private school, since their children were taught by competent teachers (themselves as parents) and given instruction for substantially the same period as the public schools while using a quality curriculum. As a result, the judge dismissed all charges, declaring the Josts were operating a bona fide private school.

In another example, the district court of Rawlins County in the *Hardon* case dismissed charges of a "child in need of care" and found the Hardons' school to be a "bona fide private school using a competent instructor as required under KSA 72-1111." The Hardons' private school, Shadow Wings Academy, had one student, the Hardons' daughter, and the teachers were the Hardons themselves.[18]

In North Carolina, the Supreme Court defined a school in the home, where only the parents were the teachers of their own children, as a legitimate private school.[19] After reviewing many cases, the Court declared:

> In summary, our sister jurisdictions, when faced with the question of whether home instruction is prohibited by school attendance statutes which specify various standards for nonpublic schools, have always analyzed the question *not in terms of any meaning intrinsic to the word "school"* but rather in terms of whether the particular home instruction in question met the statutory standards... we think this is the better approach to the problem.[20]

Whether the home school won or lost its right to operate as a private school, the specific court's reasoning, in whatever state, has

---

18. See *In the Interest of Hardon*, No. 85-JV-9 (Rawlins County Dist. Ct., January 17, 1986).
19. *Delconte* v. *State*, 329 S.E.2d 636 (N.C. 1985).
20. *Delconte*, at 644–645.

virtually always been the same; Does the home school meet the minimum standards of a private school? If the home school does, then it is a private school. If it does not, then it is not a private school.

The North Carolina Supreme Court then analyzed its legislative history and found no attempt by the Legislature to ever define the word "school." The Court concluded:

> The Legislature has historically insisted only that the instructional setting, whatever it may be, meet certain standards which can be objectively determined and which require no subjective or philosophical analysis of what is or what is not a "school."[21]

The Court stated further that a recent law passed in North Carolina to loosen restrictions on religious and private schools was evidence of the Legislature's intent to "to make it easier not harder for children to be educated in nonpublic settings." Therefore, they did not believe home schools were prohibited from operating as private schools.

This same scenario has happened in many states across the country. Most legislatures have never defined a "school" other than by listing the minimum standards a school must follow. Generally, there are no requirements that a private school have a certain amount of students or meet in a certain type of building. To try to *subjectively* define a church school as a school with more than one child, in essence, violates the laws in many states which govern church schools and private schools and contradicts the intent of the legislature.

In Texas, a landmark case was handed down by a trial court and completely affirmed by the Texas Court of Appeals and the Texas Supreme Court. The Court held that private schools which were home-based could not be discriminated against merely on the grounds they were home-based. Such discrimination is a denial of the right to equal protection under the laws.

---

21. *Delconte*, at 646.

In *Leeper* v. *Arlington Independent School District, et.al.*,[22] thousands of home schools in Texas operated as small private schools. When the private tutorial statute was repealed, home schools continued to operate as private schools. Then in 1985, the State Department of Education issued a directive declaring that it was illegal for home schools to operate as private schools. Within a short time, nearly 80 home school families across the state were hauled into court for criminal truancy charges.

At this point, Home School Legal Defense joined in with several other home school groups and brought a civil rights class action suit against the State Board of Education and every single school district. The home schoolers sought a permanent injunction to stop the prosecution, a declaration that home schools can operate as private schools, and $4 million in damages. On April 13, 1987, the home schoolers won, and the Court found that home schools which meet the minimum standards of private schools are considered legal private schools. He also placed a permanent injunction prohibiting prosecution of these private schools in the home throughout the entire state.

On page three of the opinion, the Court emphasized that the Texas legislature never defined "private or parochial" school. On page four, the Court explains that "all words and phrases in the statutes shall be construed according to the rules of grammar and common usage..." and that the "consequences of a particular construction" must be considered. On page five, the Court points out that the common usage of the word "school" in Texas always encompassed children being taught at home.

The Court concluded in its Final Judgment issued September 4, 1987, that as long as the home school had a written curriculum and taught five core subjects in a bona fide manner, it was a private school.

---

22. *Leeper*, No. 17-88761-85, Tarrant County, 17th Judicial Ct., April 13, 1987.

On November 27, 1991, the Texas Court of Appeals completely affirmed this ruling on appeal in *Texas Education Agency, et al* v. *Leeper, et al.*[23] The Court stated that the Texas Education Agency "deprived the home school parents of equal protection under the law," since their private schools in the home were unfairly discriminated against "on the sole basis of location within the home," rather than outside the home.[24]

The Court of Appeals emphasized "We therefore hold that such ground of difference does not have a fair and substantial relation to the object sought, namely, the education of all school-age children in either a public school or a private or parochial school, with the result being that *all parents* of children receiving education in private and parochial schools were not treated alike... thus depriving the home school parents of equal protection under the law."[25]

In other words, any attempt by the state to treat private schools which meet in a school building with many students differently than a private school which meets in individual homes is a denial of the parents' equal protection rights under the law. Parents who are teaching their children in compliance with the requirements and guidelines of private schools are legal. To refuse to recognize them as legal is to deny them equal protection under the law.

On June 15, 1994 the Texas Supreme Court unanimously affirmed the Court of Appeals, agreeing that a home school has the same legal status as a private school.[26]

The North Dakota Supreme Court ruled that parents still have the option to operate as a private school even though the Legislature enacted a specific home school law in *Birst* v. *Sanstead.*[27] The Supreme Court held:

---

23. *Leeper*, 843 S.W.2d 41 (Tex.App.—Fort Worth 1991).

24. *Id.,* at 51.

25. *Id.*

26. *Texas Educational Agency, et al. v. Leeper, et al.* (893 S.W.2d 432, Texas Supreme Court 1994).

27. *Birst*, 493 N.W.2d 690 (N.D. 1992).

> Nothing contained within the language of the home-based instruction exception and the private school exception indicates to us that the presumption against implied amendment or repeal has been overcome. The two provisions do not conflict or refer to each other. Neither explains that it is the exclusive exception to compulsory attendance laws for a family with a home school. In harmonizing the two provisions, we must give them both full effect. In light of the above principles, we conclude that families educating their children at home *are free to elect between the private school exception and the new home-based instruction exception to the compulsory attendance laws. The new method is not the exclusive method available for home school families.*[28]

Therefore, just because a state has passed a home school law, it does not automatically prohibit families from home schooling legally under other options of the law. Provided the home school family complies with another option under the law, they are just as legal as if they followed the home school law.

Most home school laws are not exclusive. The legislatures often never amended the requirements for private schools to exclude home-based private schools. The two options for home school parents, under either the home school law or the home-based private school law, are not in conflict with one another and must be given full effect. In *Leeper*, the Court stated that it must consider "the consequences of the particular construction." To prohibit home schools to operate as private schools would result in the prosecution of tens of thousands of law abiding citizens who follow the letter and spirit of the law and operate as private schools in Alaska, Alabama, California, Delaware, Florida, Illinois, Indiana, Kansas, Kentucky, Maine, Michigan, Nebraska, Oklahoma, and Texas. The consequences of not recognizing home schools which operate as private schools are much too severe to justify such an interpretation of the law.

---

28. *Id.*, at 695.

8 Home School Parents Have the Right to a Neutral Decision-Maker

Every state has a compulsory attendance law, and in every state the local public school officials have the exclusive authority to enforce this law. Many states give the superintendents **discretion**, in some way, over whether or not a home school will be able to operate. As a result, public school officials often treat home schooling as a privilege, not a right, which is subject to their arbitrary approval or disapproval. However, since the superintendent has a financial interest in the outcome of whether or not a home school will be allowed to operate and has a philosophical bias against home schooling, such discretion is unconstitutional as a violation of due process.

Before 1982, most state superintendents or school boards had unlimited discretion to either approve or disapprove home schools. Since then, at least thirty states have changed their laws to specifically protect home schooling, thereby reducing or eliminating the public school officials' discretionary authority.[1]

The problem of public school officials' discretionary authority over home schoolers is most apparent in the four remaining states which are classified as "approval states."[2] In most of these states

---

1. See Chapter 12 for a list of these states. For a more detailed summary of the requirements for home schoolers in all 50 states see: Christopher J. Klicka, *Home Education in the United States: A Legal Analysis*, August 2001, Home School Legal Defense Association, P.O. Box 3000, Purcellville, VA 20134.

2. Maine, Massachusetts, Rhode Island, and Utah. See Christopher J. Klicka,

home schoolers are subject to often arbitrary requirements which change from year to year at the whim of the local school officials. Home schoolers are frequently disapproved for the flimsiest reasons, such as refusing to allow a home visit or refusing to have their children tested in the public school when they have already arranged for testing privately. Another common reason is the lack of what the superintendent personally believes to be a necessary qualification. Once disapproved, the families normally face criminal truancy or "child in need of services" charges.

Even in some of the states which have passed home school laws, certain areas of the laws are still left to the discretion of the superintendent. For instance, in Florida, Virginia, and South Carolina, the superintendents have the discretion to determine if a home school child's test scores or evaluation shows "adequate" progress. In Virginia, at the end of the 1989–90 school year, one superintendent arbitrarily claimed an HSLDA member's test scores of his child were not adequate, even though over half of his public school students in the same grade scored lower. Other Virginia superintendents have arbitrarily rejected a home schooler's evaluation, completed by a certified teacher, simply by saying the progress is not satisfactory and ordering the home school to "cease and desist."

In Tennessee, the state commissioner of education has the power to waive the college degree requirement for parents who are teaching high school children and who are not supervised by a church-related school. Consistently, the commissioner uses his discretion to deny virtually every single waiver request. He does not even take into consideration the fact that many of these high school graduate parents have been successfully teaching their children at home for the last several years prior to high school.[3]

Home Schooling in the United States: A Legal Analysis, August, 1997, Home School Legal Defense Association, for more details on the approval states.

3. *Home School Court Report*, Vol. 6, No. 3, Summer edition, HSLDA, Paeonian Springs, VA.

Public School Officials Are Not Neutral Decision-Makers Regarding Home Schooling

Public School officials are not neutral when it comes to exercising their discretion and deciding whether a family should be allowed to home school. One of the most obvious reasons is that they have a **financial incentive** to disapprove a home school and thereby increase the probability that the home schooled child will be placed in the public schools. Since a local school district receives state and federal tax dollars between $2000 to $4000 per head count, 20 children being home schooled gives the school district a minimum net loss of $40,000 to $80,000 in tax money.[4] This could easily pay for another teacher's salary.

In Florida, Dan Wicklund, director of finance for the Columbia county school system explained to a reporter of the "Lake City Reporter" that he was alarmed by the amount of families home schooling (157) in his county. He said, "The county earns $2,538 per student. The total lost revenue is $398,000 for the students enrolled in home study this year."[5]

In Texas, Pat Whelan, legal counsel to the Texas Education Association bemoaned the fact that for each home school student not enrolled in the public schools, the public schools lose about $2,800 in tax money.[6]

In some states, the financial incentive is even greater. For instance, in Pennsylvania, a superintendent is encouraged by the law to make things difficult for home schoolers. Under chapter

---

4. Theodore Wade, Jr., editor, *The Home School Manual*, chapter 5, "The Battle for the Right to Teach," by Christopher Klicka (Auburn, CA: Gazelle Publications, 1988), p. 68. Also see *The Home School Court Report*, "Denying Constitutional Rights For Money," Vol. 3, No.1, Jan.-Feb. 1987.

5. "Teach Me Mom," *Lake City Reporter*, Sept. 14, 1989, p. 1-B.

6. Mark Schlachtenhaufen, "Home Schooling Under Fire," Baytown Sun, Houston, August 7, 1991.

24, section 13-1333 of the Pennsylvania Statutes, he not only has the authority to commence criminal prosecutions but also under this section, all fines imposed are collected "for the benefit of the school district in which such offending person resides." The more truancy fines filed, the more fine money the local public school receives. The home school family can avoid prosecution by enrolling in the public schools, in which case the superintendent, on behalf of the school district, receives thousands of dollars per child in increased state aid.

For instance, one HSLDA case, *Pennsylvania* v. *Hulls* involved a superintendent who continued to file charges against a family whose mother was a former public school teacher, on a weekly basis during the entire first half of the 1986–87 school year and resumed filing weekly charges during most of the 1987–88 school year. Over a two year period, the superintendent accumulated a very large financial interest in the prosecution of the Hulls. He only stopped when the compulsory attendance statute was ruled unconstitutional in regards to home schooling in *Jeffery* v. *O'Donnell*.[7]

Another reason public school officials are not neutral when making a discretionary decision concerning a home school is that many of them really believe they are the guardians of the children within the boundaries of their school district. They sincerely believe they know what is best for the children, especially since they have seven years of higher education, and the home school mother only has a high school diploma half the time.[8] With this type of bias, it is hard for many public school officials to approve home schoolers and allow them to freely operate.

---

7. *Jeffrey,* 702 F.Supp. 516 (M.D. PA 1988). For a more detailed description of the *Hull* case see "PA Victory May Come in Legislature," *The Home School Court Report*, Vol. 4, No. 3, Summer 1988, 13.

8. This description of the public school officials' mind set is based on over 2,500 conversations the author has had with school officials, while negotiating on behalf of home schoolers since 1985.

The home schools are competitors to the public schools. The more lenient the local home school policy or state law, the more families will home school their children. This is a monetary loss to the public schools and a threat to the teacher's unions. This situation where public school officials have arbitrary discretionary authority over whether home schools can freely operate is synonymous with the following hypothetical illustration. The legislature in a particular state is concerned over the quality of new cars. As a result, the legislature passes a law requiring all car dealers to be licensed. They then delegate the licensing power to the Ford dealership.

Ford is not only given the discretion to decide which car dealers should be licensed but is also given the discretion to draft its own regulations. One of the first regulations Ford naturally enacts is that all car dealers, Toyota, Chrysler, etc., can only sell cars built with Ford parts. Is the Ford dealership neutral in determining who should be licensed? Certainly no more neutral than public school officials with a vested interest in public school survival determining who should be allowed to home school.

The U.S. Supreme Court Condemns Non-Neutral Decision-Makers

The Fourteenth Amendment guarantees that life, liberty, and property cannot be taken away from an individual unless he receives "due process." This means an individual will receive certain procedural safeguards that will insure he will be treated fairly. One the elements of due process is that if an individual's liberty is at stake (in this instance, parental liberty), he has a right to be heard by a **neutral decision-maker, at the first level**. The first level for a home schooler who is being challenged is usually before the biased superintendent or school board.

The Supreme Court of the United States has definitively ruled that a decision-maker with a financial stake in the outcome is not a "neutral magistrate," and is therefore in violation of the Fourteenth Amendment Due Process Clause. In *Tumey* v. *Ohio*,[9] a mayor was the decision-maker in a process concerning a liquor law. If the mayor decided in favor of the individual, the city would receive no money. But if the mayor decided against the individual appearing before him, the mayor received a nominal sum of money, while the city received a substantial sum of money.

The Supreme Court held that **both** types of financial incentives violate the due process clause. It makes no difference if the monetary gain goes exclusively to the governmental entity (the public school), and not to the state official (superintendent). *Tumey* clearly stands for the principle that a local government official, such as a superintendent, who has a financial stake in the outcome on behalf of his local governmental unit or public school, is not a neutral decision-maker for the purpose of the Due Process Clause.

In another case, *Ward* v. *Monroeville*, the Supreme Court reaffirmed *Tumey* and made even more clear that the financial incentive need not be personal to the decision-maker. A financial incentive on behalf of his governmental unit is sufficient to violate the Due Process Clause.

> ... [T]he test is whether the mayor's situation is one which would offer a possible temptation to the average man as judge to forget the burden of proof required to convict the defendant, or which might lead him not to hold the balance nice, clear and true between the State and the accused.... [Citation omitted]. Plainly that "possible temptation" may also exist when the mayor's executive responsibilities for village finances make him partisan to maintain the high level of contribution from the mayor's court. This, too, is a situation in which an official perforce occupies two practically and seriously inconsistent positions one

---

9. *Tumey*, 273 U.S. 510 (1927).

partisan and the other judicial, [and] necessarily involves a lack of due process of law....[10]

Since the decision of the superintendent is final in most states, it cannot be argued that the decision is reviewable on appeal by a truly neutral party. However, even if some type of review were available, it would still not satisfy the Due Process Clause. The Supreme Court rejected the argument that ultimate review by a neutral decision-maker is sufficient in *Ward*, saying:

> Respondent also argues that any unfairness at the trial level can be corrected on appeal and trial de novo in the County Court of Common Pleas. We disagree. This "procedural safeguard" does not guarantee a fair trial in the mayor's court; there is nothing to suggest that the incentive to convict would be diminished by the possibility of reversal on appeal. Nor, in any event, may the State's trial court procedure be deemed constitutionally acceptable simply because the State eventually offers a defendant an impartial adjudication. Petitioner is entitled to a neutral and detached judge in the *first instance*.[11]

It is important to emphasize that home schoolers do not need to prove that the public school official disapproved the home school for the expressed purpose of receiving fine money and getting those children in his school. The home schooler need only demonstrate, according to *Ward* above that a "possible temptation" exists which "might lead him not to hold the balance nice, clear, and true" between the school district's interest as a competitor and the interest of the parents to teach their children themselves.

One federal court has commented on the application of this financial incentive/Due Process argument in an education case. The court condemned the lack of neutrality of school districts. In *Fel-*

---

10. *Ward*, 409 U.S. 57, 60 (1972).
11. *Id.,* at 61-62. [Emphasis added.]

lowship Baptist Church v. *Benton*, the federal district court stated the following in a case challenging Iowa's private education law:

> The Court cannot leave this issue without pointing out other troubling matters. There may be problems when the responsibility of determining equivalent education is placed on local school boards even when more closely defined for two reasons. First each local school board may still have a different interpretation. Second, local school boards **have an inherent conflict of interest since each student in a private school is potentially a source of additional state aid.**[12]

It is clear that the Due Process Clause is contravened when a government decision-maker can effectively put money into his official coffers by denying a parent the right of home education.

Actually, the Due Process Clause's requirement of neutrality runs deeper than just the monetary neutrality. The principle of due process is violated when the decision-maker occupies two positions—"one partisan, the other judicial."[13] It is clear that superintendents are obviously partisans of public education. Giving such a partisan total discretionary review of a competing form of education is highly suspect under the Due Process Clause. A superintendent is placed in a personal conflict when he has to rule whether a child should stay in the public school which he, with seven years of higher education, administers, or be taught at home by a mother with only a high school diploma.

State Home School Cases Requiring a Neutral Decision-maker

Only two state education cases, both in North Dakota, have ruled on the issue of whether or not a superintendent, who has a financial interest and a bias, violates due process.

---

12. *Fellowship*, 620 F.Supp. 308, 318 (S.D. Iowa 1985).
13. *Ward, supra.*

In *State* v. *Toman*, the North Dakota Supreme Court upheld a truancy conviction where a home school family asserted that the exemption provisions in the compulsory attendance law violate the Due Process Clause because they allow biased public school officials to decide whether or not to grant the requests for exemption. This Court, however, declined to rule on the merits of the Due Process argument because the family was charged before they sought the exemption from the biased school official.

> We conclude that it is unnecessary to resolve this issue on the merits, because resolution of the issue cannot constitute grounds for reversing the Toman's convictions in this case. The Tomans did not seek to obtain an exemption until December 11, 1987, subsequent to the time period of the alleged violations. Having failed to request an exemption in which the statutory violation occurred, the Tomans cannot now raise objections to the exemption statute as a defense to their convictions.[14]

The principle to learn from *Toman* is that the non-neutral decision-maker defense may be only applicable if the home school family sought the exemption and was denied **before** they were charged.

In addition, this same Court also considered this Due Process argument in another case, *State* v. *Anderson*. In this case, the Andersons argued that the law requiring them as home school parents to be certified was unconstitutional because the school board was not a neutral decision-maker, violating of the principles of due process required by the 14th Amendment to the United States Constitution. This Court **agreed** with the Andersons that,

> The Due Process Clause entitles a litigant to an impartial, neutral, and disinterested tribunal in both civil and criminal cases. *Marshall v. Jerrico, Inc.*, 446 U.S. 238, 100 S.Ct. 1610, 64 L.Ed.2d 182 (1980). Marshall v. Jerrico, Inc., 446

---

14. *Toman*, Criminal Nos. 880186 and 880187, Slip. Op. 1-2, February 10, 1989.

U.S. 238, 100 S.Ct. 1610, 64 L.Ed.2d 182 (1980);. Neutrality in adjudicative proceedings safeguards two critical concerns of procedural due process: the prevention of unjustified or mistaken deprivations and the opportunity for the individual affected by the decision-making to participate in the process with the assurance that the arbiter is not predisposed to find against him. *Id.* Thus, in *Tumey v. Ohio, supra,* the United States Supreme Court reversed criminal convictions rendered by a city judge who was also the city mayor and whose salary as mayor was paid in part by fees and costs levied by him in his judicial capacity. The Court stated that the Due Process Clause would not permit any "procedure which would offer a possible temptation to the average man as a judge to forget the burden of proof required to convict the defendant, or might lead him not to hold the balance nice, clear and true between the State and the accused." *Tumey v. Ohio, supra,* the Court invalidated a procedure by which sums produced from a mayor's court accounted for a substantial portion of municipal revenues, even though the mayor's salary was not augmented by those sums.[15]

However, the North Dakota Court did not agree that the statute was unconstitutional, because it held that the process that a school board was to follow for a private school exemption was not discretionary in nature. This Court said:

> In order to remove any doubt of due process infirmities under Section 15-34.1-03(1), N.D.C.C., we construe that provision to require the local school board to monitor whether or not a school-age child is attending a school that has been approved by the county superintendent of schools and superintendent of public instruction. The local school board's function is to monitor that attendance, and attendance at an approved private or parochial school automatically satisfies the compulsory attendance law. The

---

15. *Anderson,* 427 N.W.2d 316, 320 (N.D.) (1988) *cert. denied,* U.S., 109 S.Ct. 491 (1988).

local school board's act is a ministerial function rather than a discretionary, decision-making function and is distinguishable from the function of the mayor-city judge in *Tumey v. Ohio, supra,* and *Ward v. Village of Monroeville, supra.* We conclude that Section 15-34.1-03(1), N.D.C.C. does not violate the Due Process Clause of the United States Constitution.[16]

The principle to learn here is that the function of the decision-maker must be discretionary and not merely ministerial. In other words, if the legislature enacts a law that requires a home school parent to have a "high school diploma," the superintendent performs a ministerial function in determining whether the parent has a high school diploma. However, if a statute requires a home school parent to be "qualified," the superintendent performs a discretionary function in defining "qualified" and applying his whim to his decision. The latter would violate the due process clause.

In conclusion, school officials cannot be given the authority to decide whether or not families can teach their children at home. They have both a financial incentive and a natural partisanship or bias which precludes them from serving as a neutral decision-maker as required by the Due Process Clause.

---

16. *Id.,* 427 N.W.2d at 320.

9 The Unconstitutionality of Home Visits

Home schoolers throughout the country are frequently faced with attempts by certain school districts to unilaterally impose a "home visit" requirement. Home schoolers who refuse to allow home visits are "disapproved" and often charged with criminal truancy. Usually under a home visit "requirement," a school official will visit a home school at anytime, observe instruction in the home, inspect facilities, and demand certain changes.

All of these school districts which have home visit requirements are in states where the education statutes **do not mandate** home visits. In other words, the various state legislatures have never delegated this authority to school districts in the first place. In fact, in 1993, the only state in the entire country that actually authorized home visits by statute had its law repealed by the passage of H.B. 1260. The repeal of the home visit requirement resulted in the dismissal of a federal law suit, *Davis* v. *Newell School District* [1] in which HSLDA challenged the home visit law as unconstitutional under the 4th Amendment.

The purpose of this chapter, therefore, is to demonstrate that home visits of home schoolers should not be practiced or legislated in any state because they are inherently **unconstitutional** for four basic reasons.

---

1. *Davis* v. *Newell*, Civ. 93-5012, filed January 20, 1993 in the U.S. District of South Dakota, Western Division.

Home Visits Violate the Fourth Amendment and the Right to Privacy

First of all, home visits are a violation of the home school family's **right to privacy** and their right to be free from warrantless searches and seizures as guaranteed by the **Fourth Amendment.** On August 7, 1986, in *Kindstedt v. East Greenwich School Committee*,[2] the practice of home visits was struck down, setting precedent for the entire state. The Commissioner held in a written opinion,

> "it is our view that both the 4th Amendment and also the constitutionally derived right to privacy and autonomy which the U.S. Supreme Court has recognized, protect individuals from unwanted and warrantless visits to the home by agents of the state."[3]

Furthermore, he stated,

> "in view of the legal and constitutional considerations, we are unable to perceive any rationale whereby a home visitation requirement would be justifiable under circumstances such as these."[4]

It is clear from this decision that home visitation cannot be mandated by public school officials over parental objection. The privacy of the parents, family and home is at stake. Such privacy of the parents was protected in the United States Supreme Court in *Griswold v. Connecticut*.[5]

A school official can only inspect a home schooler's home if the family voluntarily allows them to come in or if the state official has a warrant or court order signed by a judge based on prob-

---

2. *Kindstedt* v. *East Greenwich School Committee*, slip.op. (Rhode Island Commissioner of Education, August 7, 1986).

3. *Id.*, at 5, ftn. 12.

4. *Id.*, at 7.

5. *Griswold,* 381 U.S. 479 (1965).

able cause. Any home school family who does not want to voluntarily participate in home visits cannot be required to do so without violating their 4th amendment and privacy rights.

It is a fundamental principle of due process that if a government official comes into one's home for the purpose of making a determination whether or not a criminal law is being complied with, then such an intrusion into the home is a search within the meaning of the Fourth Amendment. Since violation of the compulsory attendance law is a crime, a home visit by a public school official to determine compliance with the law is a violation of the home schooler's Fourth Amendment rights.

A home visit by a public school official to inspect a home school is equal to a "warrantless search," since it invades the privacy of the home. The U.S. Supreme Court stated: "Except in such special circumstances, we have consistently held that the entry into a home to conduct a search or make an arrest is unreasonable under the Fourth Amendment unless done pursuant to a warrant." 6 It seems apparent that home visits are unconstitutional.

Many school district officials expect their "requirement" for home visits to be complied with readily and without question. If a family will not agree to such an invasion of privacy, the school officials often wrongly assume that the home schooler is trying to hide something. School officials believe such a visit is an "inconsequential" request. However, the framers of the constitution secured, for all citizens, protection from these type of arbitrary state intrusions. The U.S. Supreme Court makes clear their intent:

> Though the proceeding in question is divested of many of the aggravating incidents of actual search and seizure, yet, as before said, it contains their substance and essence, and effects their substantial purpose. It may be that it is the obnoxious thing in its mildest and least repulsive form; but illegitimate and unconstitutional practices get their first

---

6. *Steagald* v. *United States*, 451 U.S. 204, 211 (1981).

footing in that way, namely, by silent approaches and slight deviations from legal modes of procedure. This can only be obviated by adhering to the rules that constitutional provisions for the security of person and property should be liberally construed. A closed and literal construction deprives them of half their efficacy, and leads to gradual depreciation of the right, as if it consisted more in sound than in substance.[7]

Home schoolers are constitutionally justified to refuse warrantless searches such as home visits. There is neither statutory or constitutional authorization for parents to open their houses to public school officials.

The Fourth Amendment Demand for Probable Cause

School officials are not the only officials who attempt to illegally enter the homes of home school families. Often home school families are anonymously turned over to child welfare agencies on child abuse hotlines. Nearly everyone of these referrals are false and malicious, but the social worker still has to investigate. Unfortunately, many social workers insist on entering the home and talking to the children separately. However, social workers have no more right to enter a home schooler's home than school officials unless they have a warrant based on "probable cause."

The term "probable cause" prohibits both school officials and social workers from entering home schools based on mere suspicion or an anonymous tip. In other words, "probable cause" is a high constitutional standard which puts a heavy burden on the social workers or school officials to acquire reliable evidence before they demand to inspect a home schooler's home.

---

7. *Boyd* v. *United States*, 116 U.S. 616, 635 (1886).

In the Fourth Amendment, the U.S. Constitution states:

> The right of people to be secure in their persons, houses, papers, and effects against unreasonable searches and seizures shall not be violated, and no warrants shall issue but upon *probable cause* supported by oath or affirmation and particularly describing the place to be searched and the person or things to be seized.

This language of "probable cause" has protected those accused of crimes throughout the history of our country. *Black's Law Dictionary* defines probable cause as:

> Reasonable cause; having more evidence for than against; a reasonable ground for belief in the existence of facts warranting the proceedings complained of... probable cause is the existence of circumstances which would lead a reasonably prudent man to believe in the guilt of the arrested party; mere suspicion or belief unsupported by facts or circumstances is insufficient.

Furthermore, in the famous U.S. Supreme Court decision concerning probable cause, *Wong Sun v. United States* the Court held:

> It is basic that an arrest with or without a warrant must stand upon firmer ground than mere suspicion... the quantum of information which constitutes probable cause— evidence that would warrant a man of reasonable caution in the belief that a felony has been committed—must be measured by the facts of the particular case.[8]

The U.S. Supreme Court explained further that the fundamental requirement of probable cause can never be relaxed because it would "leave law-abiding citizens at the mercy of the officer's whim or caprice." In addition, the Court explained that any evidence making up probable cause had to be either reliable evidence or from a

---

8. *Wong*, 37 U.S. 471, 1961.

reliable informant. The Supreme Court emphasized that any evidence gathered without probable cause could later be suppressed by a court of law. In other words, the burden is always on the state official to prove that he has sufficient, reliable probable cause not based on a mere suspicion.

The Home School Legal Defense Association won a landmark case before the Court of Appeals in Alabama where a home schooler was faced with an order of the court granting a social worker entrance into his home and interrogation of the children based on an anonymous tip. After HSLDA was able to obtain an injunction to stop the order from being carried out, HSLDA was also able to secure a ruling from the Alabama Court of Appeals which stated:

> We suggest, however, that the power of the courts to permit invasion of the privacy protected by our federal constitution, is not exercised except upon a showing of reasonable or probable cause to believe that a crime is being or is about to be committed ... The cause shown was unsworn hearsay and could at best present a mere suspicion. A mere suspicion is not sufficient to rise to reasonable or probable cause ... we consider that the order entered in this case was illegal.[9]

This case has essentially stopped the abuse by social workers in Alabama who are trying to enter homes or demand evidence by claiming they had sufficient probable cause since there was an anonymous tip that the home schooler or other parent was not in compliance with the law. An anonymous tip or mere suspicion is not sufficient probable cause.

As a result of the probable cause protection guaranteed by the 4th Amendment, mandating routine visits of home schools is inherently unconstitutional. School officials or social workers do not have the right to require home visits.

---

9. *H.R. v. State Department of Human Resources*, 609 S 2d 448 Alabama Court of Appeals, 1992).

Home Visits Violate the Fifth Amendment Right to Due Process

During the last several years, two states, New York and Pennsylvania, engaged in home visits of home schools even though such a requirement was not specifically mandated by law. In both states, the practice of home visits was abruptly discontinued by case precedent and subsequent legislation.

In New York, two county court decisions, *In the Matter of Dixon*, [10] and *In the Matter of Standish*,[11] both held home visits to be unconstitutional. In *Dixon*, the Court held:

> ... This Court firmly believes that the insistence of the Hannibal Central School District authorities to effect the desired on-site inspection was arbitrary, unreasonable, unwarranted, and violative of the Respondents' [home school parents] due process rights guaranteed under the Fifth Amendment of the Constitution of the U.S. The school district cannot expect to put itself in the position of conducting the inspection and then turning around and impartially or objectively determining whether the program subject to that inspection meets the required criteria for valid home instruction.[12]

Regarding protection from self-incrimination, the Court explained:

> The Respondents, further, cannot reasonably be put in a situation where they in effect are being forced to give evidence that might be used against them at a future date...[13]

The Court concluded that the home visit requirement is both "unconstitutional" and "unenforceable." This reasoning of the decision was confirmed *In the Matter of Standish*.

---

10. *Dixon,* No. N-37-86, Family Court of Oswego County, Nov. 21, 1988.
11. *Standish,* Slip. op., No. N-125-86, Oswego County, Dec. 23, 1988.
12. *Dixon, supra*, slip opinion at 5.
13. *Dixon*, at 5.

In order to cure the vagueness in the New York compulsory attendance law, the State Education Department issued "Regulations of the Commissioner of Education" for home schooling. The regulations give the local school boards no authority to conduct home visits (unless a home school is on probation), thereby ending the practice of routine home visits in the state of New York.

In Pennsylvania, at least one quarter of the 501 school districts were mandating home visits, although they were not required by law. The Home School Legal Defense Association, as a result, sued eleven school districts for violating the civil and constitutional rights of the home schoolers. The Federal Court ruled in favor of the home schoolers in *Jeffery v. O'Donnell*[14] and declared the law "unconstitutional for vagueness." The legislature subsequently passed §13-1327.1 in 1988 which ended the practice of home visits.

It is important to add that certain school districts in South Carolina also sought to impose home visits on home schoolers even though they were not mandated in the law. On February 27, 1989, the Attorney General said such a practice of mandatory home visits was prohibited by the intent of law:

> Because the amendments do not expressly provide for an on-site visit and because the only reference to the site is the "description" of the place of instruction, a reasonable reading of the whole statute (*Sutherland Statutory Construction*, Volume 2A, sec. K6.05) indicates that the legislature's intent was not to authorize blanket requirements for on-site visits.[15]

In conclusion, where home visits are not clearly mandated by law, local school district policies that have tried to impose such requirements are routinely found to be arbitrary, unreasonable, unwarranted, a violation of the Fifth Amendment, not the intent of

---

14. *Jeffery,* 702 F.Supp. 516 (M.D. PA 1988). See Chapter 6 for more details about the *Jeffery* case.

15. South Carolina OAG February 27, 1989 at 2.

the legislature, unconstitutional, and, in several instances, based on unconstitutionally vague laws.

Home Visits Fail the Compelling Interest Test

On December 16, 1998, HSLDA scored a major victory in the *Brunelle* case before the Massachusetts Supreme Judicial Court when the court struck down the public school's authority to conduct "home visits" of home schoolers. *Brunelle v. Lynn Public Schools.*[1] The Massachusetts compulsory attendance law allows for children who are "otherwise instructed in a manner approved in advance by the superintendent or the school committee." For years, home schoolers struggled against arbitrary school committee home school approval policies established in the over 300 school districts throughout the state.

The Pustell family notified the Lynn public school officials in 1991 of their intention to home educate their child. The Brunelles also notified the same school district that they would be teaching their five school age children at home. The school district reviewed both of their curricula and qualifications and found them to be satisfactory. However, they insisted that the families must "allow the superintendent to periodically . . . observe and evaluate the instructional process and to verify that the home instruction plan is being implemented in the home" in spite of their strenuous objections.

HSLDA then filed a declaratory judgment that the home visit requirement violates the home school family's rights under Massachusetts law.

In ruling in favor of the home schoolers in the *Brunelle* case, the Massachusetts Supreme Judicial Court recognized that the Massachusetts compulsory attendance law, by allowing home schooling, "protects the basic constitutional right of parents to direct the

---

1. *Brunelle*, 702 N.E.2d 1182 (1998).

education of their children."[2] Since this case involved the fundamental right of parental liberty, the court applied a "compelling interest test," which requires the court to determine whether a state regulation or policy is "essential" to fulfill the state's compelling interest in education.

In applying this standard, the court cited an earlier precedent in *The Care and Protection of Charles*,[3] that "the approval of the home school proposal must not be conditioned on the requirements that are not *essential* to the state interest in assuring that all children be educated."[4] The court reemphasized, "A home visit is not presumptively *essential* to protection of the state's interest in seeing that children receive an education, and therefore, such visits may not be required as a condition to approval of the plaintiff's plan."[5]

Furthermore, the court found there are less restrictive means of fulfilling the state's interest: "The results of their teaching programs can be adequately verified through testing without the need to visit the home to see a formal schedule is being followed."[6] The issue of privacy was also a concern of the court:

> "Both the United States Supreme Court and this court have emphasized, in connection with the protective right of parents to raise their children, that government may not intrude unnecessarily on familial privacy. *Curtis v. School Committee Falmouth*, 420 Mass. 749, (1995). This concern as well as others dictates, as we said in the *Curtis* case, that home education proposals can be made subject only to essential and reasonable requirements." Non-consensual home visits are dead in Massachusetts.

The *Brunelle* decision serves as an ominous warning to those school districts across the country that still insist on home visits. The fam-

---

2. *Brunelle*, at 1184.
3. 399 Mass. 324 (1987).
4. *Brunelle*, at 1184.
5. *Brunelle*, at 1184.
6. *Brunelle*, at 1186.

ily's right of privacy, and the recognition that home visits are not essential or the least restrictive means to fulfill the state's compelling interest, protects home schoolers from these unwanted intrusions.

Conclusion

Mandatory home visits are clearly unconstitutional for many reasons. However, if the school official or social worker has a warrant signed by a judge that allows him to come into the home, the home schooler has no choice but to allow him entrance. This is very rare, since very few school officials or child welfare workers will have probable cause to obtain warrants.

Furthermore, a home schooler can *voluntarily* allow a child welfare worker in the house, but such visits are risky and can cause untold trouble for the family. The public school official may see something in the home schooler's house or in the curriculum which he does not like, and another whole battle begins. The best policy is to avoid home visits altogether and by keeping school officials out of homes of home schoolers. It is also important to object to any legislation that would impose such a requirement.

10 The Myth of Teacher Qualifications

Most education officials publicly claim that teachers need special "qualifications" in order to be effective. As a result, public education organizations sometimes target home schoolers with legislation or an interpretation of the law which would require parents to have one of three qualifications: (1) teacher certification, (2) a college degree, or (3) passage of a "teacher's exam." Although this seems reasonable on the surface, such requirements not only violate the right of parents to teach their children as guaranteed by the First and Fourteenth Amendments, but virtually all academic research documents that there is no positive correlation between teacher qualifications (especially teacher certification requirements) and student performance.

It also seems apparent that Americans in general are seeing through the "smokescreen" of teacher qualifications. On July 23, 1991, the results of a public opinion poll were released by the Washington-based Belden and Russonello public opinion research firm. It found that three out of four Americans disagreed with the notion that teacher certification requirements in public schools assure high quality teachers. The poll also found that 71 percent do not believe the lack of teacher certification in private schools means their teachers are less qualified than public school teachers.[1]

---

1. Carol Innerst, "Parents Prefer Private Schools," *Washington Times*, July 24, 1991, p. A3.

In fact, the National Education Association and some of the other members of the educational establishment are the last groups to insist upon teacher certification and high qualification standards for home schoolers in spite of the overwhelming research and popular opinion against the need for such teaching standards.

This chapter demonstrates two major problems with mandatory teacher qualifications for home school parents: (1) mandatory teacher qualifications are not necessary for children to receive a good education, and (2) teacher qualification standards on home school parents are essentially unconstitutional. This chapter includes many summaries of research projects and opinions of professional educators which all confirm the absence of a positive correlation between teacher qualifications and student performance. It will also be made apparent that there is an obvious trend in the legislatures and the courts to abandon teacher certification or other teacher qualifications for home school parents.

Research and Researchers That Expose the Myth of Teacher Qualifications

One of the most comprehensive studies in this area was performed by Dr. Eric Hanushek of the University of Rochester, who surveyed the results of *113 studies* on teacher education and qualifications. Eighty-five percent of the studies found *no positive correlation* between the educational performance of the students and the teacher's educational background. Although 7% of the studies did find a positive correlation, 5% found a *negative impact*.[2] Those who push for legislation requiring certain teacher qualifications for home schoolers have little or no research to support the necessity of such standards. The results of these 113 studies are certainly an

---

2. Dr. Eric Hanushek, "The Impact of Differential Expenditures on School Performance," *Educational Researcher*, May 1990.

indictment on proponents of certain teacher standards for home schoolers.

Dr. Sam Peavey, Professor Emeritus of the School of Education at the University of Louisville, earned advance education degrees from Harvard (Master of Arts) and Columbia (Doctor of Education) and was involved in the preparation of thousands of prospective teachers for state certification. He has served on numerous committees and commissions dealing with the accreditation of schools and colleges. On September 30, 1988, Dr. Peavey testified before the Compulsory Education Study Committee of the Iowa Legislature on the subject of teacher qualifications, citing numerous studies. He stated:

> May I say that I have spent a long career in developing and administering programs for teacher certification. I wish I could tell you that those thousands of certificates contributed significantly to the quality of children's learning, but I cannot.... After fifty years of research, we have *found no significant correlation between the requirements for teacher certification and the quality of student achievement.*

Later in his testimony, Dr. Peavey explained that he has found only *one* valid way of identifying a good teacher:

> However, in spite of years of frustration, I am pleased to report to you there has been discovered one valid, legal, honest, professional, common-sense way to identify a good teacher. As far as I know there is only one way, and it is about time for legislators to recognize it and write it into school law. It involves a simple process. Step one is *to stop looking at the teachers and start looking at the students.* Step two is to determine how well students are learning what they are supposed to be learning. The quality of learning provides the only valid measure of the quality of teaching we have yet discovered.

Dr. Peavey concluded his testimony with practical examples of excellent student achievement results by students who were being taught by their parents, most without degrees or certificates. He explained that many studies demonstrate that home-schooled children "commonly score a year or more above their peers in regular schools on standard measures of achievement."[3]

Two education researchers, R.W. Heath and M.A. Nielson surveyed 42 studies of "competency-based" teacher education. They found that no empirical evidence exists to establish a positive relation between those programs and student achievement.[4] Four other education researchers, L.D. Freeman, R.E. Flodan, R. Howsan, and D.C. Corrigan did separate studies in the effectiveness of teacher certification requirements. They all concluded that there is no significant relation between teacher certification and teacher performance in the classroom.[5]

C. Emily Feistritzer, Director of the private National Center for Education Information, claimed in a recent interview that she does not know "of a single study that says because a teacher has gone through this or that program, he or she is a better teacher." Supporters of teacher training programs "argue eloquently that teachers need to be grounded in all of these things, but there has yet to be a study that shows that in fact is this case."[6]

John Chubb, a fellow at the Brookings Institute (a liberal think tank), extensively studied various popular reforms, including the

---

3. Dr. Sam Peavey, testimony at a hearing before the Compulsory Education Study Committee of the Iowa Legislature, September 30 ,1988. Dr. Peavey made similar statements in an interview with *Insight* magazine, September 24, 1990, p. 13, Washington D.C.

4. "The Research Basis for Performance-Based Teacher Education," *Review of Educational Research*, 44, 1974, pp. 463-484.

5. See W.R. Hazard, L.D. Freeman *Legal Issues in Teacher Preparation and Certification*, ERIC, Washington D.C. 1977; R.E. Flodan, "Analogy and Credentialing," *Action in Teacher Education*, Spring/Summer issue (1979); R. Howsam and D.C. Corrigan, *Educating a Profession*, Washington D.C., American Association of Colleges for Teacher Education, (1976).

6. "The ABC's of Reform: Give Parents a Choice," *Insight* magazine, September 24, 1990, p. 13.

push to professionalize teaching, toughen teacher certification standards, and implement more extensive teacher evaluation systems. As a result, he authored a book with Terry Moe, *Politics, Markets, and America's Schools* on the subject of reform of education. Mr. Chubb found "no correlation between student achievement and any of the variables on which school reformers have been concentrating so much time, effort, and money." He continues, "There is little reason to believe" that these actions will improve student achievement and "there is considerable reason to believe they will fail."[7]

Dr. Brian Ray of the National Home Education Research Institute released a report entitled, A Nationwide Study of Home Education: Family Characteristics, Legal Matters, and Student Achievement. This was a study of over 2000 home school families in all 50 states. The research revealed that there was no positive correlation between the state regulation of home schools and the home-schooled students' performance. The study compared home schoolers in three groups of states representing various levels of regulation. Group 1 represented the most restrictive states such as Michigan which require home schoolers to use certified teachers; Group 2 represented slightly less restrictive states including North Dakota; and Group 3 represented unregulated states such as Texas and California which have no teacher qualifications. Dr. Ray concluded:

> ... *no* difference was found in the achievement scores of students between the three groups which represent various degrees of state regulation of home education.... It was found that students in all three regulation groups scored on the average at or above the 76th percentile in the three areas examined: total reading, total math, and total language. These findings in conjunction with others described in this section, do *not* support the idea that state regulation

---

7. *Id.*, p. 17.

and compliance on the part of home education families assures successful student achievement.[8]

Furthermore, this same study demonstrated that only 13.9 percent of the mothers (who are the primary teachers), had ever been certified teachers. The study found that there was no difference in students' total reading, total math, and total language scores based on the teacher certification status of their parents:

> The findings of this study do *not* support the idea that parents need to be trained and certified teachers to assure successful academic achievement of their children.[9]

This study has been confirmed by two other studies of the qualifications of home school parents. Dr. J.F. Jakestraw surveyed the student performance of home schoolers in Alabama and reported:

> This finding suggests that those children in Alabama whose parent-teachers are not certified to teach perform on standardized achievement tests as well as those whose parent-teachers are certified to teach. Therefore, it is concluded that there is no relationship between the certification status of the parent-teacher and the home-schooled children's performance on standardized achievement tests."[10]

Jon Wartes also performed a similar study on home schoolers over three years in the state of Washington and reached the same conclusion.[11]

On the whole, home schoolers' achievements are ranked above average on standardized achievement tests as demonstrated by Dr.

---

8. Dr. Brian Ray, "A Nationwide Study of Home Education: Family Characteristics, Legal Matters, and Student Achievement," National Home Education Research Institute, Seattle, WA, 1990, pp. 53-54.

9. *Id.,* p. 53.

10. Dr. J.F. Jakestraw, "An Analysis of Home Schooling for Elementary School-age Children in Alabama, Doctoral dissertation at the University of Alabama, 1987.

11. Jon Wartes, "Washington Home School Research Project," Woodinville, WA 1987-1989.

Ray's findings in the study cited above and the numerous studies summarized in Chapter 1. Dr. Ray and others have found that only 35% of teaching mothers have a college degree or higher, yet their children score no higher on standardized achievement tests than those being taught by mothers without a college degree.

Conclusion of Research

In conclusion, nearly all existing research on teacher qualifications or state regulations demonstrates that regulations have no significant relation to student performance. In fact, teacher qualification requirements have no positive correlation with even *teacher* performance. In the end, as the Coleman Report (U.S. Office of Education, 1964) pointed out, families are the most important factors in determining a student's academic performance.

Statutory Trend Lessening Teacher Qualification Requirements

The trend across the United States is to remove all teacher qualifications standards for home schoolers. The emphasis seems to be on protecting parental rights and, in several states, focusing on student performance through an annual test or portfolio evaluation.

As of May 1997, *forty-one* states do *not require* home school parents to have *any* specific qualifications. Home schoolers in these states can home school without proof of any particular educational qualifications. In fact, of the *nine* states that do have qualification requirements, *seven* of them require only a GED or high school diploma. The states in this category are North Carolina, Ohio, Pennsylvania, Georgia, South Carolina, Tennessee, West Virginia, and New Mexico. Only North Dakota requires the passage of a "teacher's test" or a college degree. New Mexico required a bachelor's degree, but this requirement was repealed in 1992, leaving a high school diploma or GED as the standard. South Carolina also previously required a college degree or a teacher's examination, but this was struck down by the South Carolina Supreme Court in HSLDA's case *Lawrence v. South Carolina Board of Education.*[12] South Carolina now only requires a GED or high school diploma. Tennessee used to require that parents who were teaching children in high school had to have a college degree. This was amended in 1994 to allow parents to teach their high school aged children with only a high school diploma or a GED as long as they were under the supervision of a "church related school."

Michigan was the last state to require home school parents to have teaching certificates. Many states formerly had a law like Michigan's, but such teacher qualifications requirements were abandoned. On May 25, 1993, the Michigan Supreme Court struck down the teacher certification requirement as unconstitutional for all religious home schoolers in HSLDA's case, *People* v. *DeJonge.*[13] Under *DeJonge*, religious home schoolers have no qualification requirements.

Major Cases on Teacher Qualifications for Home Schools and Private Schools

Below are summaries of several cases in various states which dealt with the issue of teacher qualifications and found teacher certification requirements or college degree requirements to be excessive or unconstitutional.

In New York, according to its compulsory attendance statute in section 3204, instruction "elsewhere" must be given by a "competent" teacher. The court in the case *In re Franz*, has interpreted competent to *not* mean certified.[14] Furthermore, home school regulations adopted in June 1988 do not require home school parents to have any qualifications. Home school parents are "competent"

---

12. *Lawrence*, 412 S.E.2d 394 (1991).
13. *DeJonge*, 501 N.W.2d 127 (1993).
14. *In re Franz*, 55 A 2d 424, 427 (1977).

as long as they file a notice of intent, quarterly reports of progress, and test results every other year beginning in third grade.

New Jersey law allows "*equivalent* instruction elsewhere than at school."[15] Regarding the interpretation of the word "equivalent," the New Jersey Supreme Court in the *Massa* case stated: "... perhaps the New Jersey Legislature intended the word equivalent to mean taught by a certified teacher elsewhere than at school. However, I believe there are teachers today teaching in various schools in New Jersey who are not certified. ... Had the legislature intended such a requirement, it would have said so."[16]

Ohio law requires home school teachers to be "qualified."[17] State Board of Education regulations define "qualified" as a GED or high school diploma.[18] Prior to these regulations, in *Ohio v. Whisner,* the Ohio Supreme Court struck down Ohio's Minimum Standards which required teacher certification, stating "And equally difficult to imagine, is a state interest sufficiently substantial to sanction abrogation of appellants'[parents'] liberty to direct the education of their children."[19] The Court also pointed out that the state "*did not* attempt to justify (prove) its interest in enforcing the minimum standards (which included teacher certification requirements) as applied to non-public religious schools."[20]

On May 25, 1993, Michigan's teacher certification requirement for home school parents was struck down by the highest court in the state. The Michigan Supreme Court declared:

> In summary, we conclude that the historical underpinnings of the First Amendment to the U.S. Constitution and the case law in support of it compels the conclusion that the

15. New Jersey Statutes Annotated § 18A:38-25.
16. *New Jersey* v. *Massa*, 231 A.2d 252, 256 (1967).
17. Ohio Rev. Code Ann. § 3321.04(A)(2).
18. See Ohio State Board of Education Administrative Code Chapter 3301-34.
19. *Whisner,* 47 Ohio St.2d 181, at 214 (1976), 351 N.E. 2d 750.
20. *Id.,* at 217.

imposition of the certification requirement upon the DeJonges violates the Free Exercise Clause. We so conclude because we find that the certification requirement is not essential to nor is it the least restrictive means of achieving the State's claimed interest. Thus, we reaffirm that sphere of inviolable conscience and belief which is the mark of a free people. We hold that the teacher certification requirement is an unconstitutional violation of the Free Exercise Clause of the First Amendment as applied to families whose religious convictions prohibit the use of certified teachers. Such families, therefore, are exempt from the dictates of the teacher certification requirements.[20]

This decision vindicates the dissent in a three to three split of the Michigan Supreme Court in 1986 in a private school case involving the requirement of teacher certification. In this case, *Sheridan Road Baptist Church*, three Justices found:

... enforcement of the teacher certification requirement, as applied, is not essential to achieve the objective. Unless and until the state can show otherwise, the enforcement of the statutory teacher certification requirement, as applied, would be violative of the First *and Fourteenth Amendments*.[21]

Indiana presently allows home schools under its law which exempts children from compulsory attendance if they are "provided with instruction *equivalent* to that given in public schools."[22] A federal court in the *Mazenac* case, when trying to interpret the word "equivalent" stated "... it is now doubtful that the requirements of a formally licensed or certified teacher ... would pass constitutional muster."[23] The Court would not interpret "equivalent

---

20. *Michigan* v. *De Jonge*, 501 N.W.2d 127, 144 (1993).

21. *Sheridan Road Baptist Church* v. *Dept. of Ed.*, 396 N.W.2d 373, 421 (1986).

22. Ann. Ind. Code § 20-8.1-3-34.

23. *Mazenac* v. *North Judson-San Pierre School Corporation*, 614 F.Supp. 1152, 1160 (1985).

instruction" as requiring certified teachers because of the constitutional problems involved.

In Massachusetts, "a child who is otherwise instructed in a *manner approved in advance* by the superintendent..." is exempted from attending public school.[24] When establishing guidelines for approving home schools, the Massachusetts Supreme Judicial Court stated, in the *Charles* case, that the superintendents or local public school committees could *not* require the parents to be certified or have college degrees. The Court said: "While we recognize that teachers in public schools must be certified, certification would *not* be appropriately required for parents under a home school proposal.... Nor must parents have college or advanced academic degrees."[25] In fact, the home school mother in this case, in whose favor the Court ruled, did not even have a high school diploma.[26]

In Kentucky, home schools operate as private schools. When private schools were required to use certified teachers even though the statute was unclear, the Kentucky Supreme Court, in the *Rudasill* case, ruled that teacher certification did not apply to private schools and could not be mandated.[27]

In Hawaii, according to its regulations, "parents teaching their children at home shall be deemed *qualified* instructors."[28] In other words, parents are qualified because they are parents. No certain degrees or diplomas are necessary for the parent to be able to successfully educate his children.

In South Dakota, a child formerly was allowed to be "otherwise provided with *competent* instruction."[29] However, in 1993, that statute was amended to specifically delete the term "compe-

---

24. Ann. Law of Mass. ch. 76, §1.
25. *Care and Protection of Charles*, 504 N.E.2d 592, 602 (Mass. 1987).
26. *Id.,* 504 N.E.2d at 594, fn. 2.
27. *Kentucky State Board* v. *Rudasill*, 589 S.W.2d 877, 884 (1977).
28. Dept. of Ed. Regs. 4140.2(D)(2).
29. S.D. Cod. Laws Ann. §13-27-3.

tent," thereby removing all qualifications requirements on parents who teach their own children. Nonetheless, a safeguard remains in the statute which states "the individuals[who give instruction] are *not* required to be certified."

In North Dakota, Nebraska, and Iowa, teacher certification requirements were upheld by the courts in the *Shaver, Faith Baptist*, and *Fellowship Baptist* cases.[30] In each of these cases *no* expert testimony or evidence was given to prove teacher certification was necessary or essential for children to be educated. In fact, the state could also not prove, with evidence, that teacher certification was the "least restrictive means" for children to be educated.

Furthermore, the legislatures in all three of these states have *mooted* these cases and vindicated home schooling parents by repealing the teacher certification requirements. Nebraska and Iowa have created options in their compulsory attendance statutes to allow parents to home school *without any* qualifications. North Dakota allows parents to pass a "teacher test" in order to opt out of teacher certification.[31]

Conclusion

Educational research does not indicate any positive correlation between teacher qualifications and student performance. Many courts have found teacher qualification requirements on home schoolers to be too excessive or not appropriate. The trend in state legislatures across the country indicates an abandonment of teacher qualification requirements for home school teachers. In fact, Americans in general are realizing that the necessity of teacher qualifications is a myth. The teachers' unions and other members of the

---

30. See *North Dakota* v. *Shaver* 294 N.W. 2d 883 (1980), *Nebraska* v. *Faith Baptist Church*, 301 N.W. 2d 571 (1981), and *Fellowship Baptist Church* v. *Benton*, 815 F.2d 485 (1987).

31. See Revised Stat. of Nebraska §79-1701(3); N.D. Century Code §15-34.1-03; and Iowa H.F. 455(1991).

educational establishment make up the small minority still lobbying for teacher certification in order to protect their disintegrating monopoly on education.

11 The Rights of Handicapped Home Schoolers

Home school parents teaching children with special needs or handicaps are harassed and restricted more than other home school families. In fact, in a few states like Arkansas, anyone can home school a child, **unless** that child is designated as needing special education services. In Arkansas, the special needs child can only be home schooled if the parent has a valid special education teaching certificate.[1] As a result of this discriminatory treatment, many home schoolers with special needs children begin to think that they have less parental rights than everyone else. Constitutionally, this could not be further from the truth.

Parents with special needs children are protected by the same constitution as all other parents. Therefore, they too have the protection of the First and Fourteenth Amendment as discussed in Chapters 3 and 4.

One home school family in Colorado had their child in special needs classes in the public school. After a while, their child basically stagnated. The classroom atmosphere was horrible. The parents decided they could do a better job, so they notified the school district they were going to home school. Although it was legal to home school in the state, the local school district would not disenroll the child. They felt the child's IEP recommendation could not be fulfilled by a mere mother. They called the family nearly every

---

1. Arkansas Statutes Annotated section 80-1503.9.

week, trying to pressure them back in for more meetings and more conferences with the public school's specialists. The mother could hardly stand the intimidation and began to doubt herself. When the Home school legal Defense Association was notified, they were able to convince the school district that it was exceeding its authority.

Below is short summary of the legal rights and conflicts of parents who home school children with special needs.

The Improper Application of Federal Controls to Private Home Schools

Most home school children do not receive public school services for their handicapped children. As a result, the federal regulations through the Education of the Handicapped Act (EHA) which has recently been retitled "Individuals with Disabilities Education Act" (IDEA) simply do not apply. Such home schoolers are outside the jurisdiction of these federal regulations, since they are not receiving any service.

However, a home schooler who receives public school services for his special needs child, place themselves under the jurisdiction of the federal Education of the Handicapped Act and local state regulations which implement that Act. The IDEA funding is given to each state based on the number of special needs children and how closely the state follows the IDEA regulations. As a result, each state has passed some form of regulations to implement the IDEA requirements.

However, special needs home schoolers who want to discontinue public services (or in some instances, never asked for the service to begin with) are faced with an attempt by some state officials, superintendents and principals, to require special needs home schoolers to comply with the IDEA anyway. This action by school districts is of course improper because the IDEA was established to make *public* school services available to all children on a **voluntary** basis.

Parents who do not want the free special needs services, therefore, are not under the jurisdiction of the IDEA and should not have to abide by the federal IDEA regulations or the state's regulations which implement the IDEA rules.

The purpose and intent of the Individuals with Disabilities Education Act, described in 20 USCS §1400(d), is:

> (1)(A) to ensure that all children with disabilities have available to them a free appropriate public education that emphasizes special education and related services designed to meet their unique needs and prepare them for employment and independent living; (B) to ensure that the rights of children with disabilities and parents of such children are protected; and (C) to assist States, localities, educational service agencies, and Federal agencies to provide for the education of all children with disabilities;
>
> (2) to assist States in the implementation of a statewide, comprehensive, coordinated, multidisciplinary, interagency system of early intervention services for infants and toddlers with disabilities and their families;
>
> (3) to ensure that educators and parents have the necessary tools to improve educational results for children with disabilities by supporting systemic- change activities; coordinated research and personnel preparation; coordinated technical assistance, dissemination, and support; and technology development and media services; and
>
> (4) to assess, and ensure the effectiveness of, efforts to educate children with disabilities.

20 USC 1400(d)

Throughout the entire Act, the purpose of making **available** a free appropriate education to handicapped children is the central theme. The Act defines a "free appropriate public education" as

> special education and related services which (A) have been provided at public expense, under public supervision and

direction, and without charge, (B) meet the standards of the state educational agency, (C) include an appropriate preschool, elementary, or secondary school education in the state involved, and (D) are provided in conformity with the individualized education program required under section 614(d)(5)[20 USCS §1414(d)(5)].[2]

The intent of the Act, therefore, is to provide statutory guidelines for local public schools to make available a free public education to the handicapped. The Act is **not** a compulsory attendance statute for handicapped children. Section 1412(9)(B) only allows states to receive federal money for special education services **if** "a free appropriate public education is available for all handicapped children between the ages of three and eighteen..." Most states have compulsory ages set between ages six and sixteen. If the IDEA was a federal mandate compelling all handicapped children between the ages of three and eighteen to receive special education services, it would be in direct conflict with every compulsory attendance statute in the country.

It is clearly apparent, therefore, that parents who do **not** want to take advantage of a free public education for their handicapped child are not mandated to do so. Such a mandate would also violate the parents' fundamental right to direct the education of their children as guaranteed under *Pierce* v. *Society of Sisters*.[3] In the *Pierce* case the U.S. Supreme Court declared that parents have the right to choose a *private* educational program for their children. As a result, the Court struck down an Oregon law that mandated only public school attendance. Parents of special needs children are not required to use any public educational services. To privately educate their special needs child is the parents' choice. By doing so, they avoid the state's controls under the IDEA.

---

2. 20 USCS §1401(18).
3. 268 U.S. 510 (1925)[Also see *Meyer* v. *Nebraska*, 262 U.S. 390 (1923) and *Wisconsin* v. *Yoder*, 406 U.S. 205 (1972)]. See Chapter 3 for a full discussion of this fundamental right guaranteed by the Fourteenth Amendment.

Example of Misapplication of the Law to Home Schooling the Handicapped

In Pennsylvania, the Ehmann family withdrew their handicapped child, George, from the public schools in order to instruct him privately and voluntarily discontinued all state and federal assistance. As a result, they no longer remained under the jurisdiction of the Education of the Handicapped Act and were no longer subject to the due process procedures of 20 U.S.C. §1415. Nonetheless, the Philadelphia school district alleged the Ehmanns were still under the jurisdiction of the federal IDEA and initiated a hearing under the due process procedures of the IDEA to force the family to follow the "recommendations" of the public school special needs experts. The public school, of course, wanted the child to stay in a public school special needs class. The family, as is their right, unilaterally withdrew their child from the special needs program and home schooled him privately.

The Assistant General Counsel of the Philadelphia Board of Education asserted that the Ehmanns are **"precluded"** from removing their child from the public school placement and teaching him privately. The counsel stated,

> . . . it is our belief that the Ehmanns by their refusal to comply with federal laws and procedures enacted for the protection of handicapped children, are in violation of Pennsylvania's Compulsory Attendance Laws.

This school district was attempting to make it mandatory that a special needs child comply with federal controls even though all ties to the public school had been severed.

This author, as an HSLDA attorney, filed a brief with the independent hearing officer who was assigned to hear the case pursuant to the due process procedures of the IDEA[4] and requested the hear-

---

4. The *Ehmann* brief was also expanded and filed with the Secretary of Edu-

ing officer to dismiss the case since he and the IDEA had no jurisdiction.

This author argued that the purpose and intent of the IDEA is
not to **compel** all handicapped children to utilize federally funded
special education services but rather to make available a "free and
appropriate" education to those who **choose** to take advantage of
such federal services. The Ehmanns are **not** enrolling their child in
the public school, so the superintendent has no authority to impose
federal public school standards. Furthermore, the superintendent
has no legal authority to initiate federal due process procedures
pursuant to the IDEA because those due process procedures **only**
apply to children enrolled in **public** school programs for the handicapped children, not children being **privately** home schooled such
as the Ehmanns. The only consequence for the Ehmanns in with-
drawing their child from the special needs program in order to home
school is that they forfeit all federal and state aid.[5] HSLDA also
presented the position of the U.S. Department of Education.

cation in Pennsylvania. The brief covers much precedent and other citations in
this area.

5. In *Board of Education of the City of New York* v. *Ambach*, 612 F.Supp.
230, (D.C.N.Y.1985), a family disagreed with the public school's placement of
their handicapped child and initiated administrative proceedings. In the mean-
time, the child was enrolled in a private school. The Court held

Section 1415(e)(3) does not act to preclude parents from removing
their child from an arguably inappropriate placement, but if the parents do violate the status quo provisions of Section 1414(e)(3) and
place their child in a private school without the consent of the school
agency, they do so at their own risk.

612 F.Supp. at 234. Also see *Board of Education of E. Windsor Regional
School* v. *Diamond*, 808 F.2d 987 (3rd Cir. 1986). In the *Stemple*, *Ambach*, and
Diamond cases above, nothing was even suggested that the parents had no right
to unilaterally remove their handicapped children from the public school placement under EHA. In fact, the disputes only concerned whether or not the local
officials had to reimburse them for this choice.

In *Springdale School District* v. *Grace*, 494 F.Supp. 266 (W.D.Ark. 1980),
parents sued because they preferred to have their daughter placed in the State
School for the Deaf, while the local school district wanted the girl to be placed in
their system. The local school district prevailed when the district court held that

The U.S. Department of Education Supports Special Needs Home Schoolers

The U.S. Department of Education has confirmed that the IDEA has no jurisdiction over home schools and private schools. In a letter dated June 24, 1988, Charles O'Malley, the Executive Assistant for Private Education stated,

> there is nothing in the IDEA statute or regulations that indicates that the free and appropriate public education requirement applicable to participating states was intended to interfere with the right of parents to educate their children at home or in a private school in accordance with their State's provisions for these alternatives.[6]

Furthermore, the letter states that the IDEA was not intended to regulate schools or families who chose not to participate in public agency services. He explains that the rights of nonpublic school children and the limited obligations of public agencies for those children are defined in the IDEA regulations. However, O'Malley emphasizes,

> While these regulations define the nonpublic school child's right to participate in public agency services, they do not expand or limit a State's authority to regulate or otherwise set standards for the education of children residing in the

---

the program for the girl was "appropriate" and thus satisfied the school's legal duties to offer appropriate special education. However, the court ended its opinion by reminding the parents that if they truly thought that the other program was best for the child they could choose that on their own with their own expense. The court said:

> We also note that, upon reflection, Sherry's parents may be more desirous that their child receive the *best* instead of a mere "appropriate" scholastic exposure.

494 F.Supp., at 274. [Emphasis in original].

6. Charles J. O'Malley, Ph.D., Executive Assistant for Private Education, United States Department of Education, Washington D.C., Letter to Michael P. Farris, June 24, 1988, p. 1.

State whose parents choose to enroll them in nonpublic educational programs.[7]

In other words, the IDEA standards for an appropriate education do **not** apply and were not **intended** to apply to handicapped children in home schools and private schools who do not participate in public agency services.

Ehmann Decision in Favor of Parents' Rights

The independent hearing officer refused to grant HSLDA's motion to dismiss and ruled against the family and in favor of the public school's definition of an "appropriate" education for this special needs child.

This author appealed to the Secretary of Education of Pennsylvania, Thomas K. Gilhool and he ruled in favor of the Ehmanns, granting the motion to dismiss on June 9, 1989.[8] He ordered that the hearing officer's findings of fact and conclusions of law be rejected and vacated.[9] He also ordered the school district and the family to proceed under the Pennsylvania compulsory attendance act; not the federal EHA procedures.[10]

Conclusion

Home schooling special needs children takes a tremendous effort on behalf of parents. HSLDA receives regular reports of the consistent success these parents are achieving; oftentimes far beyond the progress the special needs child made in the public school. In

---

7. *Id.,* at 2.

8. *In re the Educational Assignment of George E.*, Special Education Opinion No. 353, Dept. of Ed. of Pennsylvania, June 5, 1989, p. 3.

9. *Id.,* at 3.

10. *Id.*

fact, many learning disabilities or handicaps are conquered in the home setting. One of the major reasons for success seems to be the fact that parents know their children best and therefore, can best meet the needs of their handicapped child.[11]

Home school parents who do not use the special needs services of the local public school have the same rights as any other private home school family. Therefore, school districts are prohibited from imposing federal education standards and regulations on these families since they are outside the jurisdiction of the federal government and receive no public education funding.

---

11. See study by Dr. Steven F. Duvall, school psychologist, entitled "The Effects of Home Education on Children with Learning Disabilities," August 30, 1994. This study demonstrates that uncertified parents have more success teaching children with learning disabilities than conventional public schools do. (Study is available from HSLDA, Paeonian Spring, Va.)

12 Legislative Trends to Protect Home Schoolers

Home schooling has been operating in the United States since America's inception. However, with the advent of the public schools and subsequent compulsory attendance laws enacted primarily in the 1900s, home schooling nearly died out. In the 1980s, however, home schooling experienced a rebirth in popularity as hundreds of thousands of families diligently began teaching their own children at home. This rekindling of a historical system of education continues to grow at a tremendous pace with no sign of slowing down.

The legal road to home school, however, has not been easy, since most states did not formally recognize the right of parents to home school their own children. In 1980, only three states in the entire country — Utah, Ohio, and Nevada — officially recognized the right to home school in their state statutes. In most states, it was "open season" on families teaching their children at home, and they were often prosecuted under criminal truancy laws and educational neglect charges. Due largely to the efforts of the Home School Legal Defense Association, founded in 1983, and the willingness of many families to stand on their convictions, all this has changed. Home schooling is now clearly legal in all fifty states.

A Summary of the Home School Laws

A short summary of the home school legislation and case precedent will reveal the national trend to limit state controls over private education in favor of expanding parental liberty.

Since 1982, thirty-five states have changed their compulsory attendance law and four State Boards of Education have amended their regulations to specifically allow for home schooling with certain minimal requirements. It is important to notice that many of these states mentioned above abandoned prior statutory requirements that all teachers, including home schooling parents, to be certified because it infringed on parental rights and offered no guarantee as to the quality of education.[1] As described in Chapter 10, Michigan is the most recent state to reject teacher certification as a requirement for home schools.

A close review of these new home school laws reveals a trend across the nation to lessen state control over private forms of education.

As of May 1997, there are thirty-seven states that **by statute**, specifically allow "home instruction" or "home schooling," provided certain requirements are met. These states are Alaska, Arkansas, Arizona, Connecticut, Colorado, Delaware, Georgia, Hawaii, Florida, Iowa, Louisiana, Maine, Maryland, Michigan, Minnesota, Missouri, Mississippi, Montana, New Hampshire, New Mexico, New York, Nevada, North Carolina, North Dakota, Ohio, Oregon, Pennsylvania, Rhode Island, South Carolina, Tennessee, Utah, Virginia, Vermont, Washington, Wisconsin, West Virginia, and Wyoming.[2]

---

1. Some of these states include Colorado, Florida, Nebraska, North Dakota, Iowa, New Mexico, Virginia, and Washington.

2. See generally Christopher Klicka, *Home Schooling in the United States: A Legal Analysis*,[Purcellville, VA: Home School Legal Defense Association (HSLDA), 2001], for further specific statute citation and a complete analysis of all the home school requirements. This publication is updated every August and is available from HSLDA (540-338-5600), www.hslda.org.

At least six of these thirty-seven compulsory attendance statutes merely require home schoolers to submit an annual notice of intent verifying that instruction will be given in certain core subjects for the same amount of days as the public schools. These states are New Mexico, Nevada, Montana, Wyoming, Mississippi, and Wisconsin. In Alaska, Missouri and Michigan the home schooler does not have to notify at all. These states tend to be "model" laws since they are properly based on the "honor system" which protects parental liberty and takes all monitoring power from the state authorities. Parents are presumed to be educating their children and therefore will be left alone unless the state has evidence the children are not being educated. In Chapter 1, the tremendous academic "track-record" of home schoolers is well-established by scores of studies.

Colorado and Georgia have similar laws to the six "notification" states mentioned above, but the parents are required to have the children tested every other year. However, the test scores do not have to be submitted to the public schools.

In Virginia, Maryland, Vermont, and Tennessee, the home school laws include options for families to obtain religious exemptions from various compulsory attendance requirements.[3] For instance, in Maryland and Tennessee, home schools can choose to be supervised by churches or church schools instead of by the local public school authorities. In Vermont, home school parents can be exempted from aspects of the home school law which violates "deep religious convictions."

In Virginia, a school board "shall excuse from attendance at school any pupil who, together with his parents, by reason of bona fide religious training or belief, is conscientiously opposed to attendance at school." This means home school parents who have these bona fide religious beliefs, shall be exempt from *all* compulsory

---

3. *Id.* also see Virginia Code 22.1-257(A)(2), Maryland Regulations Code Title 13A, sections 10.01-05, Vermont Statutes Annotated Title 16, section 166b(j), and Tennessee Code Annotated section 49-6-3050(a)(2).

attendance requirements. In *Johnson* v. *Prince William County School Board*,[4] the Virginia Supreme Court clarified the law stating that "the sole test is the bona fides of their (home school family's) religious beliefs." The state's interest in education cannot be considered because the state has legislatively waived that right. In other words, the state's compelling interest burden never needs to be reached. Hundreds of religious home schoolers enjoy this freedom and the latest study shows that children under religious exemption are averaging in the 89th percentile on standardized achievement tests.

In several states where home schools are recognized as private schools, parents who are home schooling, for religious reasons, are properly protected. For example, in 1983, Alabama amended its compulsory attendance law exempting all schools operated as a ministry of a church or denomination to be exempt from all teacher certification requirements and accreditation requirements.[5] Thousands of home schools are operating as ministries of local churches or denominations and thus are exempt from onerous teacher certification requirements.

In addition, two more states, Alaska and Nebraska, amended their private school statutes in 1984 allowing for any private schools to opt out of accreditation and certification requirements by asserting sincerely-held religious beliefs.[6] Home schoolers in these two states now have the option to freely operate under these religious exemptions.

---

4. *Johnson*, 404 S.E.2d 209 (1991).

5. Alabama Code sections 16-28-1(2) through 16-28-8.

6. See Alaska Statutes §§14.45.100 through 14.45.140 (1984) and Revised Statutes of Nebraska §79-1701(2). Prior to 1984, Nebraska had been prosecuting private schools and home schools across the state who refused to use certified teachers. Pastor Sileven of Faith Baptist Church Academy was jailed and his school padlocked. An appointed Governor's Commission investigated the problem and recommended that the legislature pass an exemption for these religious schools to protect the parent's constitutional rights. The legislature adopted the recommendation into law.

In Michigan, the state supreme court in *DeJonge v. Michigan*[7] exempted all religious home schoolers from teacher certification.

The rest of these home school statutes have an additional requirement that home schoolers administer an annual standardized achievement test or have an evaluation performed which shows the child has made adequate progress. Tennessee, for example, requires that home schooled children be tested in grades 2, 3, 6, 8, and 10. West Virginia mandates that students be tested annually and achieve above the 40th percentile. Oregon requires that home schoolers score in the 15th percentile, while Minnesota requires the 30th percentile. Colorado requires only the 13th percentile and Virginia requires the 23rd percentile. Arkansas requires that children score no lower than eight months below grade level.

All of these thirty-seven home school states allow parents with only high school diplomas or less to teach their children at home except North Dakota which requires parents to take a teacher test.

States Where Home Schools Can Operate as Private Schools

The rest of the states have no specific statutes referring to home instruction, although **all states allow home schooling** under certain conditions. For example, in at least twelve states, home schools may presently operate as private schools.[8] In all of these states,

---

7. *DeJonge*, 501 N.W. 2d. 127 (1993).

8. Those states are Alabama, Alaska, California, Illinois, Indiana, Kansas, Kentucky, Louisiana, Michigan, Nebraska, Pennsylvania, and Texas. In at least six other states, groups of home schoolers qualify as private schools even though the instruction individually takes place in each home. These six states are Colorado, Florida, Maine, South Carolina, Virginia, and Utah. See Klicka, *Home Schooling In the United States: A Legal Analysis*, published by the Home School

home schoolers need only provide instruction in certain core subjects for the same time as public schools. Essentially no other requirements apply. Although each year certain school districts challenge the right of home schools to exist as private schools in these states, home schoolers have thus far been successful. Chapter 7 discusses many court cases throughout the country where home schools have been recognized as private schools.

States Where Home Schools Are Subject to Discretionary State Approval

Only four states still require that home schools be approved by the local school superintendent or school board in order to legally operate. These "approval states" also overlap into a couple of the "home school" states cited above.[9]

These "approval states", however, have somewhat vague requirements for home schoolers. Of course, each school district in these states creates its own arbitrary definition of these terms, resulting in great disparity between school districts. In Massachusetts, for example, one school district a home schooler may be completely legal but when he moves into the neighboring school district with different standards, that same home schooler is prosecuted. Other home school families have legally and successfully home schooled in one district for several years but a new superintendent comes to office, changes the rules, and criminally prosecutes the family. In fact, the vagueness in these "approval state" statutes has caused several states to abandon their approval requirements altogether, in favor of having home schoolers file notices of intent and taking standardized tests.

Legal Defense Association for an annually updated summary of the cases and statutes in these states which allow for home schools to operate as private schools.

9. See *Id.* for a complete description of these state laws. These states are Maine, Massachussetts, Rhode Island, and Utah.

The "vagueness defense" discussed in Chapter 6 and the "neutral decision-maker" problem discussed in Chapter 8 directly apply to these type of states and are used frequently to defend the rights of parents to teach their children at home.

Oklahoma Is the Only State with a Constitutional Amendment Protecting Home Schools

Home schooling is provided for in the Oklahoma constitution with no real authority being granted to the state legislature to regulate home schooling. In Article 13, section 1, it states:

> The Legislature *shall* establish and maintain a system of free public schools wherein all the children of the state *may* be educated.

This, in effect, grants the state the authority to regulate *only* public schools. In fact, in Article 13, section 5, it states: "The supervision of instruction in the public schools shall be vested in a Board of Education, whose powers and duties shall be prescribed by law." According to the Constitution, the Board of Education has no authority to regulate private or home education.

In Article 13, section 4, the Oklahoma constitution declares:

> The Legislature *shall* provide for the compulsory attendance at some public *or other school*, *unless other means of education are provided*, of all children in the State who are sound in mind and body, between the ages of eight and sixteen, for at least three months each year.

Reading these three sections together, it is clear that children "may" be educated in the public school, attend private school, *or* attend no school, as along as other means of education is provided. Under this provision, home schools could qualify as either an "other school" or as "other means of education." The term "other school" refers to all types of private schools. Since neither the constitution nor the statutes define "other school," parents educating their children could possibly qualify as an "other school." In many states throughout the country, as mentioned above home schools are legally considered private schools.

It seems quite evident, however, that the "other means of education" language is more directly applicable to home schooling since it was added for the specific purpose of protecting the right of parents to choose home schooling. In 1907, during the Oklahoma Constitutional Convention, one of the delegates, Mr. Buchanan, proposed that the phrase "unless other means of education be provided" be added to Article 13, section 4. Favorably responding to Mr. Buchanan's proposal, another delegate, Mr. Baker stated,

> "I think Mr. Buchanan has suggested a solution. A man's own experience sometimes will teach him. I have two little fellows that are not attending a public school because it's too far for them to walk and *their mother makes them study four hours a day.*"

As a result, of this discussion on home schooling, the "other means of education" language was added to Article 13, section 4.

This means that the framers of the Oklahoma Constitution specifically intended to preserve the right of parents to educate their own children at home. Furthermore, it seems apparent that according to the Constitution, no powers were granted to the state legislature or department of education to restrict or regulate home schooling.

Trend Toward Lesser State Control of Home Schooling

In conclusion, all the cases and amended statutes mentioned above, and many dozens more, point to a trend in the courts and legislatures for less state control of home education. Constitutionally, the state only has an interest in the **product** of education, not the **process.** Whenever the state attempts to control the **process** of education, such as dictating teacher qualifications, approving curriculums, or requiring home visits, it is at loggerheads with parental liberty. On the other hand, if the states pass laws concerning the **product** of education, such as various notification requirements or, perhaps, standardized testing, the parents' rights and the state's interests can be peacefully balanced.

Appendix I
Home School Students
Excel in College

Are well-rounded, talented, even academically excellent students encountering cumbersome technical difficulties when they apply at your college or university? This summer, a 16-year-old in Texas made a perfect SAT score.[1] A student in Maryland came within 10 points of perfection, but restrictive admission requirements may cause trouble for them — they are both home educated.[2]

The standardized test results of over 16,000 home educated children, grades K-12, were analyzed in 1994 by researcher Dr. Brian Ray. He found the nationwide grand mean in reading for home schoolers is at the 79th percentile; for language and math, the 73rd percentile. This ranking means home educated students perform better than approximately 77% of the sample population on whom the test was normed. Nearly 80% of home schooled children achieve individual scores above the national average and 54.7% of the 16,000 home schoolers achieved individual scores in the top quarter of the population, more than double the number of conventional school students who score in the top quarter.[3]

---

1. June 11, 1996, San Angelo, TX, *Standard-Times*, article by Ron Durham about Travis Brown.

2. March 15, 1996, *The Baltimore Sun*, article by Edward Lee about Joshua D. Wentz.

3. *Home Schoolers Score Significantly Above National Average*, National Center for Home Education Press Release, December 7, 1994.

The current estimate of home educated students in the United States is 1.23 million to 2 million and growing. Every year a significant portion of these students seek higher education. Individualized training with its creative alternatives cannot be measured accurately by traditional transcripts. Grades are unnecessary and class rank is irrelevant. So how are admissions officers supposed to deal with these unusual cases?

The 1996 Survey of Admission Policies

This fall the National Center for Home Education (NCHE) conducted a nation-wide college survey; a sampling of the home school admission policies in all fifty states. Only 44% had verbal or written policies for home school applicants. NCHE's liberal definition of "policy" includes colleges that take into account home schoolers' unique capabilities and circumstances. Nevertheless, 96% of the colleges polled had at least one and sometimes over 200 home educated students enrolled at their college. Course descriptions or portfolios are accepted in lieu of an accredited diploma or GED by 93% of the schools polled. Several colleges had home schoolers excelling in their honors programs.

On May 10, 1994, the Wall Street Journal reported:

> Many colleges now routinely accept home-schooled students, who typically present "portfolios" of their work instead of transcripts. Each year **Harvard University** takes up to 10 applicants who have had some home schooling. "In general, those kids do just fine," says David Illingworth, senior admissions officer. He adds that the number of applications and inquiries from home schoolers is "definitely increasing."

A Positive College Experience

The survey of over 60 colleges and universities in all fifty states conducted by the National Center for Home Education revealed the following anecdotal accounts of home schoolers in college:

A **Harvard University** admissions officer said most of their home educated students "have done very well. They usually are very motivated in what they do." Results of the SAT and SAT II, an essay, an interview, and a letter of recommendation are the main requirements for home educated applicants. "[Transcripts are] irrelevant because a transcript is basically a comparison to other students in the school."

In addition to Harvard, prominent schools like **Yale, Princeton, Texas A&M, Brown University**, the **Carnegie Mellon Institute**, the Universities of **Arizona, Maryland, Virginia, Hawaii** and many others all have flexible transcript criteria, accept parental evaluations, and do not require any accreditation or a General Equivalency Diploma (GED). At **Kansas State University** and others like **Lipscomb University** and **Middlebury College** transcripts are optional.

Birmingham-Southern College had only one home school applicant this year, but the admissions officer said the college "would be glad to have many more just like him!"

Roughly 50 home schoolers attend the **University of Montana**. "The home schoolers in this state seem to be up to date and well organized. We even have home schoolers in our honors programs. I know of one student for sure. She is one of our top students," remarked one admissions official.

Bruce Walker at the **University of Delaware** said one home educated student who "had an exceptional SAT score was invited to be considered for a full ride scholarship!"

"Home schooling is becoming more and more prevalent," said Mark Wheeler of **Boise State University**. "We're all trying to work together." **Pennsylvania State University** had 20 home school applicants in 1995, double the previous year. They prefer a portfolio with as much information as possible, including extra curricular activities that demonstrate leadership. "Home schoolers show strongly in that," said the admissions officer for Penn State.

Lewis and Clark College has a method of application called the "Portfolio Path" where a student can bypass standardized tests and instead be "reviewed on a myriad of things that would point to, and measure academic performance." The Universities of **Minnesota** and **Mississippi** also look at the all-around abilities demonstrated in a home schooler's portfolio. **University of Kentucky** home school applicants "have to provide a portfolio of what they have done throughout their high school years" that is "creative and informative." A UK admissions officer also said, "Our home schoolers (about 50) tend to be very bright, and have scored very high on standardized tests."

The **Dartmouth College** admissions officer explained, "The applications I've come across are outstanding. Home schoolers have a distinct advantage because of the individualized instruction they have received."

University of Alaska/Fairbanks has had over 300 home educated students in the last few years, several of which were in their honors program. The program director, Mary Dicicco commented, "They have been wonderful students on the whole. Tess was a marvelous student!"

Staff from **Geneva College** (PA) and **Belhaven College** (MS) are actively recruiting home schoolers by going to home school conferences and book fairs to talk to parents and students about admissions.

"Home schoolers have to work harder thereby increasing student productivity," Jeff Lantis said of the 75-90 home schoolers at **Hillsdale College** (MI). "Home schoolers are consistently among our top students, in fact home schoolers have won our distinct Honors Program the last three years in a row. We tend to look very favorably upon home schoolers applying to our college."

USA TODAY reported on October 28, 1996, that the **University of North Carolina**-Chapel Hill's dean of admissions, James Walters, has enrolled about 20 home educated students, all of which "are performing above average academically."

A letter sent in 1990 to home school leaders in Massachusetts from George A. Schiller, Jr., Director of Admissions at **Boston University** is another example of the recognition institutions of higher learning are showing home schoolers' academic achievements:

"Boston University welcomes applications from home schooled students. We believe students educated at home possess the passion for knowledge, the independence, and the self-reliance that enable them to excel in our intellectually challenging programs of study."

How are Home Schoolers Scoring on College Entrance Exams?

We knew home schoolers on average, do better on national standardized achievement tests for the elementary and secondary grade levels. Now recent statistics released find that home schoolers, on average, are above the national average on their ACT scores.

The ACT High School Profile Report of the home school graduating class of 1996, which comprised 2,369 students, the students on average scored 22.5. In 1997, another profile report was made of the results of 1,926 home school graduates and found that home schoolers maintained the average of 22.5.

This is higher than the national average of 20.9 in 1996 and 21.0 in 1997. The perfect score for the ACT is 36.

The 1996 ACT results showed that in English, home schoolers scored 22.5 compared to the national average of 20.3. In math, home schoolers scored 19.2 compared to the national average of 20.2. In reading, home schoolers outshone their public school counterparts 24.1 to 21.3. In science, home schoolers scored 21.9 compared to 21.1.

The conclusion is obvious: home schooling works!

Home Schoolers at College:
How are they doing?

The *U.S. News & World Report* reported on December 9, 1991 that an "estimated 50 percent of home-schooled students attend college, about the same rate as their public-school counterparts." How are home schoolers performing in college? "[A]s well as, if not better than, their conventionally educated counterparts," was the report from a study conducted through **Bob Jones University** (SC).

Paulo de Oliveira, Ed.D., Dr. Timothy Watson, and Dr. Joe Sutton studied 789 students and discovered that college freshmen who had completed their entire high school education in a home school had a "slightly higher overall...critical thinking score" than students educated in public or private schools. This offers "strong validation that home education is a viable and effective educational alternative."[4]

Rhonda Galloway, Ed.D., joined Dr. Sutton to compare college aptitude and found that "home schooled students demonstrate similar academic preparedness [and] achievement in college as students who have attended conventional schools." They concluded that, consistent with the success of home schoolers at the elementary and secondary levels, "home schooled students can perform adequately in the different, and more advanced, academic setting of college-level study."[5]

Many Christian colleges are rushing to obtain more home school applicants because they find the home schooled student generally has a strong Christian foundation and excels academically. For instance, an investigation conducted in the Fall of 1994 by Mike

---

4. National Home Education Research Institute (Salem, OR), *Home School Researcher*, Vol. 10, No. 4, 1995, p. 6.
5. *Ibid.*, Vol. 11, No. 1, 1995, p. 7.

Mitchell, dean of enrollment management of **Oral Roberts University** (OK) discovered that 212 home schooled students were enrolled at ORU which is about 10% of the student body. The average home schooler had an above average ACT score of 24.0 and SAT score of 1005. The study showed that although home schoolers had virtually the same ACT/SAT average as the ORU student body, they had a statistically higher cumulative GPA at ORU. The average ORU GPA is 2.76 while the average ORU home schooler GPA is 3.02.[6]

Furthermore the study revealed that 88% of ORU home schooled students were involved in one or more outreach ministries. Many of the home schoolers serve as Chaplains in the dorms and virtually all embrace the Honor Code as an already adopted way of life. In addition, over 90% of ORU home schoolers are involved in intramural sports and nearly 80% are involved in various campus clubs and organizations. Home schoolers are active in all areas of college life.

- *1997 Galloway/Sutton Study*

On October 10, 1997 the results of a four-year study was released by Drs. Rhonda Galloway and Joe Sutton. The purpose of conducting the study was to find out how home schoolers fared in the college setting as compared to Christian and public school graduates. The study tracked 180 students, 60 graduates from home schooling, public school, and Christian school. Five success indicators were used in the study: Academic, Cognitive, Spiritual, Affective-Social, and Psychomotor.

Galloway and Sutton found that in every success category except psychomotor, the home school graduates excelled above the other students. Out of 12 academic indicators, the home schoolers ranked first in 10. Out of 11 spiritual indicators, home schoolers

---

6. *Home Schoolers At Oral Roberts University*, a study conducted in the fall of 1994 at Oral Roberts University, 7777 S. Lewis Ave., Tulsa, OK 74171.

ranked first in seven. In cognitive skills, home schoolers ranked first in 17 of the 23 indicators. Out of 63 total indicators, home schoolers ranked first in 42.

Home School Scholarships

As a result of the above study, Oral Roberts University created a unique Home School College Preparatory Program and established a $6,000 scholarship especially for home school graduates, above and beyond all other financial aid.

Eager to attract these bright young students, other colleges are developing Home School Scholarships. **Belhaven College** grants $1,000 a year to qualified home educated students. **Nyack College** (NY) says their "experience with home schoolers has been a positive one" and awards up to $12,000 to home schoolers. **Liberty University** (VA) recognizes the "hard work, dedication, and self-motivation behind your success in home education" and also extends "a $12,000 scholarship."

Home Educated Athletes

According to The Chronicle of Higher Education, June 7, 1996, the National Association of Intercollegiate Athletics and the National Christian College Athletic Association both have guidelines for home schoolers. This year, the National Collegiate Athletic Association (NCAA) drew up new "guidelines to help standardize eligibility for home-schooled athletes. According to the guidelines, home-schooled athletes who have sufficiently high standardized-test scores and proof that they took at least 13 courses that meet the association's core-course standards may be automatically awarded freshman eligibility." An NCAA spokeswoman said that from 1988 to 1993, as many as 10 home-taught athletes applied for waivers each year. "In each of the past three years," she said, "that number has grown to more than 20."

How Are Colleges Recruiting Home Schoolers?

- by attending state home school conventions and making specialized presentations,
- developing college preparatory programs targeted at home schoolers,
- sponsoring on-campus recruitment activities and visitation opportunities,
- communicating regularly with state-wide home school organizations,
- joining in on home school radio network broadcasts,
- conducting workshops for home schoolers and their parents to help them plan for college admission (like Penn State's Home Schooling High Schoolers Conference),
- offering special scholarships,
- and advertising in brochures and home school publications like *Teaching Home*, *Practical Home Schooling*, *Home Schooling Today*, and other magazines.

National Center for Home Education Recommendations

Home educated high school graduates offer an academically and socially creative background. Home schoolers also tend to exhibit "a strong work ethic" and have high moral values which contribute to their success in college. More and more colleges and universities are recognizing their unique capabilities and circumstances. In light of the proven success of home education at the elementary, secondary, and post-secondary levels, we recommend colleges adopt specific written home school admission policies which reflect the following:

1. Should home educated applicants be required to submit an accredited diploma or GED? No, accreditation does nothing to measure a student's knowledge or what he was taught, it only reflects *where* he was taught. A GED carries with it the stigma of being a high school drop-out. Home schoolers are not drop-outs, but talented, conscientious students who have completed their high school education. They should not be treated as drop-outs by being required to obtain a GED.

2. If a transcript is required, colleges should have flexible guidelines for records and documentation of the basic credit hours for high school completion. Some colleges supply home schoolers with a "Home School Credit Evaluation Form" that may be completed in lieu of a transcript.

3. As the primary instructors, parents should be recognized as capable of evaluating their student's academic competence for letters of recommendation. Schools frequently ask for an additional evaluation from someone outside the home.

4. SAT/ACT scores and portfolios or performance-based assessments provide schools with a solid basis for admission. Like most colleges, the University of Missouri-Columbia relies heavily on test results and the dozen or so home schoolers they have in every freshman class "tend to have excellent test score results." In addition, UMC emphasized a GPA is "not a factor in admitting home schoolers."

5. Mandatory SAT II testing in specific subjects is an unnecessary road block. Requiring only home school students to take these tests, in addition to the SAT, is discriminatory. Colleges will discourage home schoolers from seeking admission by holding them to this unreasonable standard.

SAT/ACT testing is more than enough to show academic levels.

6. A bibliography of high school literature and an essay are two admission criteria for accurately evaluating a student's exposure and thinking skills. "These home schoolers write fabulous essays!" said Emory University "Very creative!"

7. Extracurricular activities and interviews are two of the best ways to focus on overall student proficiency and leadership qualities.

For more information contact the Home School Legal Defense Association at 540-338-5600 or review HSLDA's webpage at www.hslda.org.

Appendix II
Why Do We Need State
Parental Rights Acts?

Parental rights are under siege. Parents, in many ways, are becoming "second class citizens" as lower courts elevate the power of the state to supersede the wisdom of parents. Parental choice is in jeopardy. Freedom is at stake. The basic fundamental freedom of parents to raise their children hangs in the balance. Have we forgotten whose children they are anyway? They are a God-given responsibility to parents.

Earlier this century, the United States Supreme Court declared "The child is not the mere creature of the state; those who nurture him and direct his destiny have the right and high duty to recognize and prepare him for additional obligations." – *Pierce* v. *Society of Sisters* [268 U.S. 510 (1925)].

In 1972, in *Wisconsin* v. *Yoder* (406 U.S. 205), the Court described parental rights as fundamental, saying: "This primary role of the parents in the upbringing of their children is now established as an enduring American tradition."

The U.S. Supreme Court has repeatedly recognized that the liberty clause in the 14th Amendment guarantees the fundamental right of parents to direct the education and upbringing of their children. Below are several more examples of the U.S. Supreme Court recognizing parental rights as fundamental.

The **Fourteenth Amendment guarantees the right of the individual**... to establish a home and bring up children, to worship God according to his own conscience. — *Meyer v. Nebraska*, 262 U.S. 390, 403, (1923)

[W]e think it entirely plain that the Act of 1922 unreasonably interferes with **the liberty of parents** and guardians to direct the upbringing and education of children. — *Pierce v. Society of Sisters*, 268 U.S. 510, 534, (1925)

Thus a state's interest in universal education, however highly we rank it, is not totally free from a balancing process when it impinges on **fundamental rights** and interests, such as those specifically protected by the Free Exercise Clause of the First Amendment, and the traditional interest of parents with respect to the religious upbringing of their children.... This case involves the fundamental and religious future and education of their children. — *Wisconsin v. Yoder*, 406 U.S. 205, 214, (1973)

The **fundamental liberty interest** of natural parents in the care, custody, and management of their child does not evaporate simply because they have not been model parents or have lost temporary custody of their child to the state.... — *Santosky v. Kramer*, 455 U.S. 745, 753, (1982)

The Court has recognized that the freedom to enter into and carry on certain intimate or private relationships is a **fundamental element of liberty** protected by the Bill of Rights... the intimate relationships to which we have accorded Constitutional protection include marriage... the begetting and bearing of children, child rearing and education. — *Board of Directors of Rotary International v. Rotary Club of Duarte*, 481 U.S. 537, 545, (1987)

[T]he Court has found that the relationship of love and duty in a recognized family unit is an interest in **liberty entitled to Constitutional protection**....— *Lehr v. Robertson*, 463 U.S. 248, 258, (1983)

Although the U.S. Supreme Court clearly recognizes parents' rights as fundamental and thus protected by a higher standard of review, many lower courts over the last twenty-five years have eroded this traditional view of parental rights. A parental rights act will reaffirm parents' rights, including the fundamental rights to make medical decisions, discipline, and direct the education and religious training of their children.

Furthermore, a parental rights act will mandate that courts apply the "compelling interest test" (*i.e.* "strict scrutiny standard"), requiring the state to prove that its regulation and infringement of parental rights is *essential* and the *least restrictive means* of fulfilling the state's compelling interest.

Below are some examples of what happens when lower courts ignore U.S. Supreme Court precedent in not recognizing parents' rights as fundamental or entitled to the protection of the compelling interest test. In many ways, these decisions or state actions reduce children to being "mere creatures of the state." You be the judge!

• Eleven-Year-Old Pennsylvania Girls Subjected to Gynecological Exams (1996)

On March 19, 1996, fifty-nine sixth graders in Pennsylvania's East Stroudsberg Area School District were forced to strip to their underwear and submit to a full genital examination. Many of these eleven-year-old girls objected to the exam, and, weeping, asked for permission to call their parents. School officials ridiculed the students, calling them "babies" and refusing to allow them to contact their parents. A nurse blockaded the door, preventing the girls from leaving. The exam left many of the children devastated and feeling violated.

School officials defended their actions by arguing that they sent notices to the parents. However, the notices never indicated that a gynecological exam would be performed. At least one parent objected in writing to the exam, but her child, who now is experiencing nightmares from the incident, was forced to strip and submit to examination. One pediatrician summed up the school's position, stating, "Even a parent doesn't have a right to say what's appropriate for a physician to do when they are doing an exam." Several parents are considering filing suit for violation of their parental and civil rights. (Sources: "Anger Mounts on Exams of Genitals," by Tara Gravel, *The Pacini Record*, March 26, 1996; "School Exams by Pediatrician Upset Parents," *The Associated Press*, March 28, 1996; "Middle-School Genital Exams Criticized," by Chary Weltzstein, *The Washington Times*, May 5, 1996.)

• *Brown v. Hot, Sexy and Safer, Inc.*, 68 F.3d 525 (1st Cir. 1995)

Parents in Chelmsford, Massachusetts were never told that their children would be required to sit through a ninety-minute presentation by "Hot, Sexy and Safer Productions, Inc." In this so-called "group sexual experience," a male child was told to lick a condom, after which a female student was told to pull the condom over his entire head and blow it up! The Court of Appeals held that the parent's rights were not violated because the actions were not sufficiently "conscience shocking." The court further held that even if under *Meyer* and *Pierce* the right of parents to direct the upbringing of their children is fundamental, it does not encompass a broad-based right to restrict this form of information from their children in public schools.

• *In re Sumey*, 94 Wash.2d. 757, 621 P2d. 108 (1980)

In this case the Supreme Court of Washington ruled that it was not a violation of constitutional parents' rights to remove a child from the home because she objected to her parents' reasonable rules. The parents had grounded their eighth grade daughter because she wanted to smoke marijuana and sleep with her boyfriend. The Supreme Court found that it was reasonably within the lower court's jurisdiction to remove the girl from her family home. No strict standard was applied. The parents' rights were completely terminated for simply grounding their daughter to stop her from using illegal drugs and engaging in illicit sex!

• *People* v. *Bennett,* **501 N.W.2d 106 (Mich. 1993)**

In the case of *Michigan* v. *DeJonge*, 501 N.W.2d 127 (Mich. 1993), the Michigan Supreme Court held that parents who home educate their children due to their religious convictions have a fundamental right protected by the First Amendment. Given those facts, the State had to prove that a teacher certification requirement was necessary to achieve a compelling state goal before it could restrict a parental right. The State was not able to justify such a burden, so the religiously motivated home schoolers won.

In *Bennett,* the companion case to *DeJonge,* a family challenged the same law deemed a violation of the DeJonge family's parental rights. The court rejected the Bennett's challenge, holding that mere parental rights as guaranteed by the 14th Amendment could be infringed by any rule that was rationally related to a legitimate state purpose. In other words, the courts did not recognize parental rights under the 14th Amendment as fundamental. As a result, the court reasoned, the strict scrutiny standard, which applied to the Christian parents in *DeJonge* did not apply to the secular parents in *Bennett*. In other words, parental rights of religious parents are protected but the parental rights of secular parents are not protected!

• *Ohio Association of Independent Schools* v. *Goff,* **92 F. 3d 419 (6th Cir. 1996)**

In this case, the U.S. Sixth Circuit Court of Appeals rejected the request of an association of independent schools to enjoin the State of Ohio from revoking their charter because the school association did not require its students to take outcomes based tests. The state of Ohio argued that a parent had a "limited right, if any, to direct the secular education of his or her children secured by the Fourteenth Amendment."

The Court agreed and crushed the parents' rights. The Court concluded that secular parental rights do not receive protection of the "compelling interest test" standard of review. The Court ruled,

> The Supreme Court has applied strict scrutiny to such Fourteenth Amendment claims where they are coupled with a challenge based on the Free Exercise Clause of the First Amendment. *Yoder*, 406 U.S. at 233, 92 S.Ct at 1542. Absent a free exercise challenge, however, the Court has applied rational basis review, noting that parents have no constitutional right to "private school education unfettered by reasonable government regulation." *Runyon*, 427 U.S. at 178, 96 S.Ct. At 2598.

This is an example of a court ruling that the parents' right to direct secular education is not protected.

• *Immediato* v. *Rye Neck School District*, 73 F.3d 454 (2nd Cir. 1996).

In another very similar case, the United States Court of Appeals held that parents who objected on moral grounds to a mandatory community service graduation requirement did not have a fundamental right to direct the education of their children. The court held that the moral concerns of the parents were purely secular and not religious in nature. The court indicated its belief that the **Supreme Court has never expressly indicated whether the right of a parent to direct the upbringing of a child is "fundamental"** and thus deserving of strict scrutiny when invoked against a state regulation.

• *Herndon* v. *Chapel Hill-Carrboro City Board of Education*, 89 F.3d 174, (4th Cir. 1996)

Parents objected to a school graduation requirement that forced the children to perform certain community service projects. The Fourth Circuit Court held "Because plaintiffs' objection to the program arises out of purely secular concerns, the right asserted by the plaintiff parents in this case is not a fundamental right." The court held that the state's right to direct the secular education of a child are superior to the rights of the parents as long as it is rationally related to a legitimate governmental interest.

- *Cornwell v. State Board of Education,* **314 F.Supp. 340 (D.Md. 1969)**

  aff'd. 428 F.2d. 471 (4th Cir.1970), cert. den. 400 U.S. 942 (1970)

  When Maryland required every elementary school to provide comprehensive sex education for all students, parents went to federal court demanding an "opt-out" provision. The judge dismissed all their claims outright. The court avoided properly applying the compelling interest test.

- *Bendiberg v. Dempsey,* **707 F.Supp. 1318 (N.D.Ga. 1989)**

  The United States District Court held that a father's rights were not violated when a county department of family and children services removed a son from his care, without prior notice or opportunity for a hearing, after the father refused consent to the insertion of a catheter for the administration of prescribed medication. The court found that the parents rights to make medical decisions for the child had not been violated even though the attending physician indicated that the patient's condition did not constitute a medical emergency.

- *In re Sampson,* **65 Misc.2d 658, 317 N.Y.S.2d 641 (Fam.Ct. 1970)**

  aff'd. 377 App.Div.2d 668, 323 N.Y.S.2d 253 (1971), *aff'd.* 29 N.Y.S.2d 900, 278 N.E.2d 918, 328 N.Y.S.2d 686 (1972).

Kevin, age fifteen, had "elephant man disease," which caused a large fold of skin to grow over the right side of his face. Kevin's mother wanted to wait until Kevin turned twenty-one before permitting any surgery. The doctors testified that the surgery was very risky, and offered no cure, and that waiting would decrease, not increase the risk. Even so, the judge overruled the mother's objections, declared Kevin a "neglected child," and ordered the series of operations.

- ***Bailey v. Menzie*, 542 N.E.2d 1015 (Ind. App.1989)**

This is an example of a case in which a state court explicitly acknowledged that parental rights were a fundamental liberty deriving from the 14th Amendment, **but incorrectly applied a reasonable relations test rather than the compelling interest test to the state action.** The court merely gave "lip service" to parental rights as fundamental.

- ***American Academy of Pediatrics* v. *Van de Kamp*, 214 Cal.App.3d 831 (San Francisco Sup. Ct., 1989)**

aff'd sub nom. American Academy of Pediatrics v. *Lungren*, 26 Cal.App.4th 479 (Ct.App. 1994).

After the U.S. Supreme Court ruled that states could require parental consent before a minor's abortion, California enacted exactly what the Court had permitted. Abortion activists filed suit against the law in a San Francisco courthouse, which ruled that under the California constitution, a child's privacy right outweighed any fundamental right of parents to know.

- ***Care of Protection of Charles*, 504 N.E.2d 592 (1987)**

In this case the Supreme Judicial Court of Massachusetts upheld a law requiring an "approval process" for home schools, ruling against parents asserting violation of their 14th Amendment parental rights. The Court did not require the state to prove, with evidence, that the approval process was the least restrictive means as required by the compelling interest standard.

• *Maine v. McDonough,* **468 A. 2d.** 977 (1983)

The Supreme Judicial Court of Maine ruled against the parents who asserted that their 14th Amendment parental rights were being violated by the onerous home school regulations. The Court did not apply a strict scrutiny standard. Instead, they evaluated the regulations by a reasonableness standard.

• *Hanson v. Cushman,* **490 F.Supp. 109 (1980)**

• *Clonlara v. Runkel,* **722 F.Supp. 1442 (E.D. Mich. 1989)**

In both of these cases, the U.S. District Courts ruled that the **parents' right to direct the education of their children was not a fundamental right.** Therefore, the plaintiff parents, in both of these cases, were not entitled to the protection of the compelling interest standard. Their parental rights had to submit to "reasonable government regulations."

• *United Nations Convention on the Rights of the Child* **(CRC)**

President Clinton has ordered the U.S. to sign the CRC. The treaty would give children fundamental rights which could be legally enforceable against parents. Because the U.S. Constitution declares treaties to be a source of supreme law, the treaty would undermine the rights of parents to direct the education and religious training of their children, make medical decisions for their children, or to use reasonable corporal discipline. The U.N. Committee on Children, which officially interprets the meaning of this treaty, has ruled that it requires Britain to outlaw corporal punishment, conduct public educational campaigns to cause society to accept the prohibition of corporal punishment, limit the rights of parents to withdraw their children from sex education classes, and change laws to increase the ability of children to participate in their parents decisions concerning them. *Concluding Observations of the Committee on the Rights of the Child: United Kingdom,* CRC/C/15/Add.34 (Jan. 1995).

The move to ratify the CRC evidences further attempts to destroy parental rights in America. State parental rights acts, on the other hand, would end the erosion of parental rights.

States Need to Act

The above contains a sampling of reported cases over the past two decades where courts have usurped the traditional role and fundamental rights of parents. Our parental liberty is guaranteed by the 14th Amendment; yet many lower courts continue to erode the U.S. Supreme Court's decisions in this area.

There is a parental rights movement across the states which is advancing the cause of parental freedom and stopping the progress of the anti-family/child's rights movement. Below is model language to be used when seeking to pass a parental rights act in a state legislature or a constitutional amendment to a state constitution. Also, there is the language from three states, Kansas, Michigan, and Texas that have formally passed parental rights acts. HSLDA working to pass acts or amendments in more states.

State Parental Rights Amendments and Acts

• **Model Language for States: Two Strategies**

    1. **Constitutional Amendment or Act**

The right of parent to direct the upbringing and education of their children is a fundamental right.

[optional: The state maintains a compelling interest in the investigating, prosecuting, and punishing child abuse and neglect as defined by statute.]

2. **Attorney fees for certain civil rights including parental rights (as introduced as SB 612 in Virginia in 1998)**

   If, in a civil case, a state trial court enters an order finding that an officer or employee of the Commonwealth, a locality, as defined in §15.2-102, or an officer or employee of a locality or any agency thereof, has taken action which deprives any natural person of life, liberty, or property without due process of law, or which denies to any natural person within its jurisdiction the equal protection of the law, including actions which (i) discriminate on the basis of race, religion, or sex or (ii) violate fundamental rights and duties of a parent to direct the upbringing and education of his or her child, then the court shall allow such party denied or deprived, if represented by counsel, a reasonable attorney's fee.

- **States That Have Passed Parental Rights Acts**

  ◊ **Michigan**
  M.C.L.A. §380.10. It is the natural, fundamental right of parents and legal guardians to determine and direct the care, teaching, and education of their children.

  ◊ **Kansas**
  K.S.A. Sec. 159(b). Parents shall retain the fundamental right to exercise primary control over the care and upbringing of their children in their charge.
  (c). Any parent may maintain a cause of action in a federal or state court, or before an administrative tribunal of

appropriate jurisdiction for claims arising under 42 U.S.C. 1983 and any damages resulting therefrom or arising under the principles established in subsection (b).

(d). Upon the finding by the court of a substantial basis for claim, the court shall award attorney fees to the parent.

◊ **Texas**

Tex. Gen. Laws 102 (1997), mandates that the Child Protective Services *"shall not contradict the fundamental rights of parents to direct the education and upbringing of their children."*

Tex. Gen. Laws 1225 (1997): "No state agency may adopt rules or policies or take any other action which violates the fundamental right and duty of parents to direct the upbringing of the parents' child."

Appendix III
Religious Freedom
Loses Ground — But
States are Fighting Back

On June 25, 1997, the U.S. Supreme Court, by a 6-3 majority, ruled the Religious Freedom Restoration Act (RFRA) unconstitutional in *City of Boerne* v. *Flores*. After the city of Boerne denied a building permit to a church because the church building was located in a historic district, Catholic Archbishop Flores of San Antonio appealed this decision based on his belief that this denial of the church's right to expand to accommodate its growing congregation violated the RFRA.

• History of the RFRA

The RFRA was originally drafted in response to a 1990 Supreme Court decision (*Smith II*) in which the Court gave the lowest level of protection to religious liberty—one of the foundational freedoms of home schooling. Using this ruling, a state could override an individual's right to freely exercise his religious beliefs merely by proving that its regulation was "reasonable."

HSLDA helped form the coalition which drafted and promoted the RFRA. Three years later, Congress passed the RFRA and President Bill Clinton signed it into law, reversing the disastrous effects of *Smith II* by restoring religious freedom as a fundamental right.

The RFRA affirmed a 1963 decision (*Sherbert v. Verner*) in which the Supreme Court held that in order for a state's regulation to prevail over an individual's right to freely exercise his religious belief, the state had to prove that its regulation was essential to achieve a compelling interest. In addition, the state had to provide evidence that it was using the least restrictive means to accomplish this compelling interest. Under this high standard of review, religious freedom was usually upheld over restrictive state regulations.

However, in the *City of Boerne* case, the Supreme Court held that the power of Congress under Section 5 of the 14th amendment is limited to "enforcing the provisions of the Fourteenth Amendment." In the Court's opinion, Congress does not have the authority to determine what constitutes a constitutional violation. The Court held that the RFRA went too far in attempting to change the substantive law of constitutional protections. According to the *Boerne* decision, Congress can make determinations as to the proper interpretation of the Constitution, but courts ultimately have the authority to determine if Congress has exceeded its own constitutional bounds. In other words, the Supreme Court, not Congress, is the final arbiter in interpreting the Constitution.

Unfortunately, Justices Rehnquist, Scalia, and Thomas—joined with the majority in knocking our First Amendment right down from its lofty fundamental right status to a simple garden variety category. The court ruled that only when a person's claim to freely exercise a religious belief is combined with another fundamental right still receiving the protection of the compelling interest test (in a "hybrid situation") such as freedom of speech, freedom of the press, or the fundamental right of parents to direct the education and upbringing of their children, will it be given more than a simple "reasonableness test."

Dissenting in the minority with Justices Breyer and Souter, Justice O'Connor stated that the Court should have used this case to revisit the *Smith* decision of 1990 since *Smith* had so drastically redefined the standard of review of the Free Exercise Clause, departing from decades of Supreme Court precedent.

[T]he Court's rejection of this principle in *Smith* is supported neither by precedent nor as discussed...by history. The decision has harmed religious liberty. The historical evidence casts doubt on the Court's current interpretation of the Free Exercise Clause.

O'Connor gave a stirring review of the importance of religious freedom in our country, quoting a number of state religious freedom charters. She noted that

early in our country's history, several colonies acknowledged that freedom to pursue one's chosen religious beliefs was an essential liberty. Moreover, these colonies appear to recognize that government should interfere in religious matters only when necessary to protect the civil peace or to prevent licentiousness.

She further explained that every state constitution included the right to freely exercise religious beliefs. She quoted James Madison and Thomas Jefferson in summary, explaining,

To Madison, then, duties to God were superior to duties to civil authorities — the ultimate loyalty was owed to God above all...the idea that civil obligations are subordinate to religious duty is consonant that government must accommodate, where possible, those religious practices that conflict with religious law."

O'Connor concluded,

It has long been the Court's position that freedom of speech — a right enumerated only a few words after the rights to Free Exercise — has a special Constitutional status. Given the centrality of freedom of speech and religion to the American concept of personal liberty, it is altogether reasonable to conclude that both should be treated with the highest degree of respect...The rule the Court declared in *Smith* does not faithfully serve the purpose of the Constitution. Accordingly, I believe it essential for the Court to reconsider its holding in *Smith*."

• States Enacting Religious Freedom Acts

In 1993, HSLDA and a broad coalition of organizations worked very hard to get the RFRA enacted. This coalition is now regrouping, to urge all of the 50 states to pass their own Religious Freedom Act to counter the *Boerne* case's devastating impact on religious freedom.

Also home schoolers have helped pass religious freedom acts in New Mexico, Alabama, Florida, South Carolina, Arizona, Illinois, and Texas. HSLDA drafted and lead the efforts to pass RFRAs in Oklahoma and Idaho. Rhode Island and Connecticut were the first to pass Religious Freedom Acts.

The following language of SB1394 in Idaho, which was enacted on March 31, 2000, is carefully crafted and can serve as model language to introduce in other states:

IDAHO SENATE BILL NO. 1394

Be It Enacted by the Legislature of the State of Idaho:

Title 73, Idaho Code, is amended by adding a new chapter, to be known and designated as Chapter 4, Title 73, Idaho Code, and to read as follows:

FREE EXERCISE OF RELIGION PROTECTED

73-401. DEFINITIONS. As used in this chapter unless the context otherwise requires:

(1) "Demonstrates" means meets the burdens of going forward with evidence, and persuasion under the standard of clear and convincing evidence.

(2) "Exercise of religion" means the ability to act or refusal to act in a manner substantially motivated by a religious belief, whether or not the exercise is compulsory or central to a larger system of religious belief.

(3) "Government" includes this state and any agency or political subdivision of this state.

(4) "Political subdivision" includes any county, city, school district, taxing district, municipal corporation, or agency of a county, city, school district, or municipal corporation.

(5) "Substantially burden" means to inhibit or curtail religiously motivated practices.

73-402. FREE EXERCISE OF RELIGION PROTECTED.

(1) Free exercise of religion is a fundamental right that applies in this state, even if laws, rules or other government actions are facially neutral.

(2)Except as provided in subsection (3) of this section, government shall not substantially burden a person's exercise of religion even if the burden results from a rule of general applicability.

(3) Government may substantially burden a person's exercise of religion only if it demonstrates that application of the burden to the person is both:

(a) Essential to further a compelling governmental interest;

(b) The least restrictive means of furthering that compelling governmental interest.

(4) A person whose religious exercise is burdened in violation of this section may assert that violation as a claim or defense in a judicial proceeding and obtain appropriate relief against a government. A party who prevails in any action to enforce this chapter against a government shall recover attorney's fees and costs.

(5) In this section, the term "substantially burden" is intended solely to ensure that this chapter is not triggered by trivial, technical or de minimis infractions.

73-403. APPLICABILITY.

(1) This chapter applies to all state laws and local ordinances and the implementation of those laws and ordinances, whether

statutory or otherwise, and whether enacted or adopted before, on or after the effective date of this chapter.

(2) State laws that are enacted or adopted on or after the effective date of this chapter are subject to this chapter unless the law explicitly excludes application by reference to this chapter.

(3) This chapter shall not be construed to authorize any government to burden any religious belief.

73-404. SEVERABILITY.

If any provision of this act or its application to any person or circumstance is held invalid, the invalidity does not affect other provisions or applications of this act that can be given effect without the invalid provision or application and to this end the provisions of this act are severable.

Appendix IV
Cases Supporting the Least Restrictive Means Component of the Compelling Interest Test

Least Restrictive Means

"Requiring a State to demonstrate a compelling interest and show that it has adopted the **least restrictive means** of achieving that interest is the most demanding test known to constitutional law."

City of Boerne v. *Flores*,
1997 US Lexis 4035, 46

"When the State enacts legislation that intentionally or unintentionally places a burden upon religiously motivated practice, it must justify that burden by 'showing that it is the **least restrictive means** of achieving some compelling state interest.'"

Church of Lukumi Babalu Aye v. *Hialeah*,
508 U.S. 520, 578, (1993)

"Court recognized the State's interest in restricting the ballot to parties with demonstrated public support, the Court took the requirement for statewide contests as an indication that the more onerous standard for local contests was not the **least restrictive means** of advancing that interest."

Norman v. *Reed*,
502 U.S. 279, 292, (1992)

"[T]he Court of Appeals concluded that it was unclear whether Resolution 66-156 directly advanced the State's asserted interests and whether, if it did, it was the **least restrictive means** to that end."

Board of Trustees of the State Univ. of New York v. Fox,
492 U.S. 469, 473, (1989)

"The Government may, however, regulate the content of constitutionally protected speech in order to promote a compelling interest if it chooses the **least restrictive means** to further the articulated interest."

Sable Communis. of California, Inc. v. FCC,
492 U.S. 115, 126, (1989)

"[H]e contends that the State must establish that the disclosure requirement directly advances the relevant governmental interest and that it constitutes the **least restrictive means** of doing so."

Zauderer v. Office of Disciplinary
Counsel of the Supreme Court of Ohio,
471 U.S. 626, 650, (1985)

Appendix V
The United States
Supreme Court
Describing the
Compelling Interest
Test: the "Essential" or
"Necessary" Component

"The state may justify a limitation on religious liberty by showing that it is **essential** to accomplish a overriding government interest."

United States v. Lee,
455 US 252, 257, (1982)

"The Court of Appeals found the injunction to be content based and neither **necessary** to serve a compelling interest nor narrowly drawn to achieve that end."

Madsen v. Women's Health Center,
512 US __, __, (1994)

"[W]e think it clear that a government regulation is sufficiently justified... if the incidental restriction on the alleged First Amendment freedom is no greater than is **essential** to that [governmental] interest."

Barnes v. Glen Theatre Inc.,
501 US 560, 567, (1991)

"For the state to enforce a content-based exclusion it must show that its regulation is **necessary** to serve a compelling state interest and that it is narrowly drawn to achieve that end."

Perry Ed. Assn. v. Perry Local Ed. Assn.,
460 US 37, 45, (1983)

"It [the university] must show that its regulation is **necessary** to serve a compelling state interest and that it is narrowly drawn to achieve that end."

Widmar v. Vincent,
454 US 263, 270, (1981)

"[The] appellees were exercising a constitutional right, and any classification which serves to penalize the exercise of that right, unless shown to be **necessary** to promote a compelling government interest, is unconstitutional."

Shapiro v. Thompson,
394 US 618, 634, (1969)

"[W]e think it clear that a government regulation is sufficiently justified...if the incidental restriction on the alleged First Amendment freedom is no greater than is **essential** to that [governmental] interest."

United States v. O'Brien,
391 US 367, 377, (1968)

Appendix VI
Troxel v. Granville:
A Victory for
Parental Rights

On June 5, 2000, the United States Supreme Court issued a landmark opinion on parental liberty. The decision was *Troxel v. Granville* 530 U.S. 57 (2000). In this case, Jennifer and Gary Troxel petitioned a Washington Superior Court for the right to visit their grandchildren against the wishes of the parents. They used as their authority a section of the Revised Code of Washington, which permitted "any person may petition the court for visitation rights at any time including, but not limited to, custody proceedings. The court may order visitation rights for any person when visitation may serve the best interests of the child, whether or not there has been any change of circumstances."

The U.S. Supreme Court ruled in favor of the parents, determining that the Washington statute "unconstitutionally interferes with the fundamental right of parents to rear their children." This decision affirmed the Washington Supreme Court. The Court ruled that "no court has found that Granville was an unfit parent. That aspect of the case is important, for there is a presumption that fit parents act in the best interest of their children." The Court went on to cite their earlier decision of *Parham v. J.R.*, 442 U.S. 584 at 602 (1979). The Court explained that this presumption that parents are fit parents means that "so long as the parent adequately cares for his or her children (i.e., is fit), there will normally be no reason for the state to inject itself into the private realm of the family to further question the ability of that parent to make the best decisions concerning the rearing of that parent's children."

The error in the Superior Court's decision to grant the petition of visitation to the grandparents was that he placed on the parent, the fit custodial parent, the burden of "disproving that visitation would be in the best interests of her daughters." The U.S. Supreme Court held that on the contrary, the grandparent must rebut the presumption that the parent's decision to refuse the grandparent visitation was reasonable and within their ability as a fit parent to make the best decisions concerning their children.

The U.S. Supreme Court cited a long history of their decisions upholding parental rights as fundamental. The Fourteenth Amendment provides that no State shall "deprive any person of life, liberty, or property, without due process of law." We have long recognized that the Amendment's Due Process Clause, like its Fifth Amendment counterpart, "guarantees more than fair process." *Washington v. Glucksberg, 521 U.S. 702, 719, 138 L. Ed. 2d 772, 117 S. Ct. 2258 (1997).* The Clause also includes a substantive component that "provides heightened protection against government interference with certain fundamental rights and liberty interests." *521 U.S. at 720;* see also *Reno v. Flores, 507 U.S. 292, 301-302, 123 L. Ed. 2d 1, 113 S. Ct. 1439 (1993).*

The liberty interest at issue in this case—the interest of parents in the care, custody, and control of their children—is perhaps the oldest of the fundamental liberty interests recognized by this Court. More than 75 years ago, in *Meyer v. Nebraska, 262 U.S. 390, 399, 401, 67 L. Ed. 1042, 43 S. Ct. 625 (1923),* we held that the "liberty" protected by the Due Process Clause includes the right of parents to "establish a home and bring up children" and "to control the education of their own." Two years later, in *Pierce v. Society of Sisters, 268 U.S. 510, 534-535, 69 L. Ed. 1070, 45 S. Ct. 571 (1925),* we again held that the "liberty of parents and guardians" includes the right "to direct the upbringing and education of children under their control." We explained in *Pierce* that "the child is not the mere creature of the State; those who nurture him and direct his destiny have the right, coupled with the high duty, to recognize and prepare him for additional obligations." *268 U.S. at 535.* We returned to the subject in *Prince v. Massachusetts, 321 U.S. 158, 88 L. Ed. 645, 64 S. Ct. 438 (1944),* and again confirmed that there is a constitutional dimension to the right of parents to direct the upbringing of their children. "It is cardinal with us that the custody, care and nurture of the child reside first in the parents, whose primary function and freedom include preparation for obligations the state can neither supply nor hinder." *321 U.S. at 166.*

In subsequent cases also, we have recognized the fundamental right of parents to make decisions concerning the care, custody, and control of their children. See, *e.g.,* *Stanley v. Illinois, 405 U.S. 645, 651, 31 L. Ed. 2d 551, 92 S. Ct. 1208 (1972)* ("It is plain that the interest of a parent in the companionship, care, custody, and management of his or her children 'comes to this Court with a momentum for respect lacking when appeal is made to liberties which derive merely from shifting economic arrangements'" (citation omitted)); *Wisconsin v. Yoder, 406 U.S. 205, 232, 32 L. Ed. 2d 15, 92 S. Ct. 1526 (1972)* ("The history and culture of Western civilization reflect a strong tradition of parental concern for the nurture and upbringing of their children. This primary role of the parents in the upbringing of their children is now established beyond debate as an enduring American tradition"); *Quilloin v. Walcott, 434 U.S. 246, 255, 54 L. Ed. 2d 511, 98 S. Ct. 549 (1978)* ("We have recognized on numerous occasions that the relationship between parent and child is constitutionally protected"); *Parham v. J. R., 442 U.S. 584, 602, 61 L. Ed. 2d 101, 99 S. Ct. 2493 (1979)* ("Our jurisprudence historically has reflected Western civilization concepts of the family as a unit with broad parental authority over minor children. Our cases have consistently followed that course"); *Santosky v. Kramer, 455 U.S. 745, 753, 71 L. Ed. 2d 599, 102 S. Ct. 1388 (1982)* (discussing "the fundamental liberty interest of natural parents in the care, custody, and management of their child"); *Glucksberg, supra*, at 720 ("In a long line of cases, we have held that, in addition to the specific freedoms protected by the Bill of Rights, the 'liberty' specially protected by the Due Process Clause includes the right... to direct the education and upbringing of one's children" (citing *Meyer* and *Pierce*)). In light of this extensive precedent, it cannot now be doubted that the Due Process Clause of the Fourteenth Amendment protects the fundamental right of parents to make decisions concerning the care, custody, and control of their children.

The U.S. Supreme Court finally held, "Considered together with the Superior Court's reasons for awarding visitation to the Troxels, the combination of these factors demonstrate that the visitation order in this case was an unconstitutional infringement on Granville's fundamental right to make decisions concerning the care, custody, and control of her two daughters."

Justice Thomas, in his concurring judgment, indicated that the plurality appropriately recognized a parental liberty. He explained further that strict scrutiny needed to be applied to infringements of these type of fundamental rights.

Parents battling oppressive state regulations and invasions of their families have a clear decision which upholds their parental rights.